KB092060

# Discover Korean

**Discover Korean _ KOREA 101**



First Published and distributed in 2019
by Pagijong Press, Inc.
4, Cheonho-daero 16ga-gil, Dongdaemun-gu,
Seoul, Republic of Korea 02589
**Tel** : 82-2-922-1192
**Fax** : 82-2-928-4683
www.pjbook.com

**Publisher** : Park Chan-ik

**ISBN** 979-11-5848-518-4 13710

Printed in Korea

* Audio files for this volume may be downloaded on the web in MP3 format at **http://www.pjbook.com/customer_download**

KOREA 101

# Discover Korean

Kyungsook Kim, Jooyeon Kang, Jin Mi Kwon,
Byung-Geuk Kim, Hwaja Park, Hyechung Cho, Hyeon Ho Lee
English editor: Terry Nelson

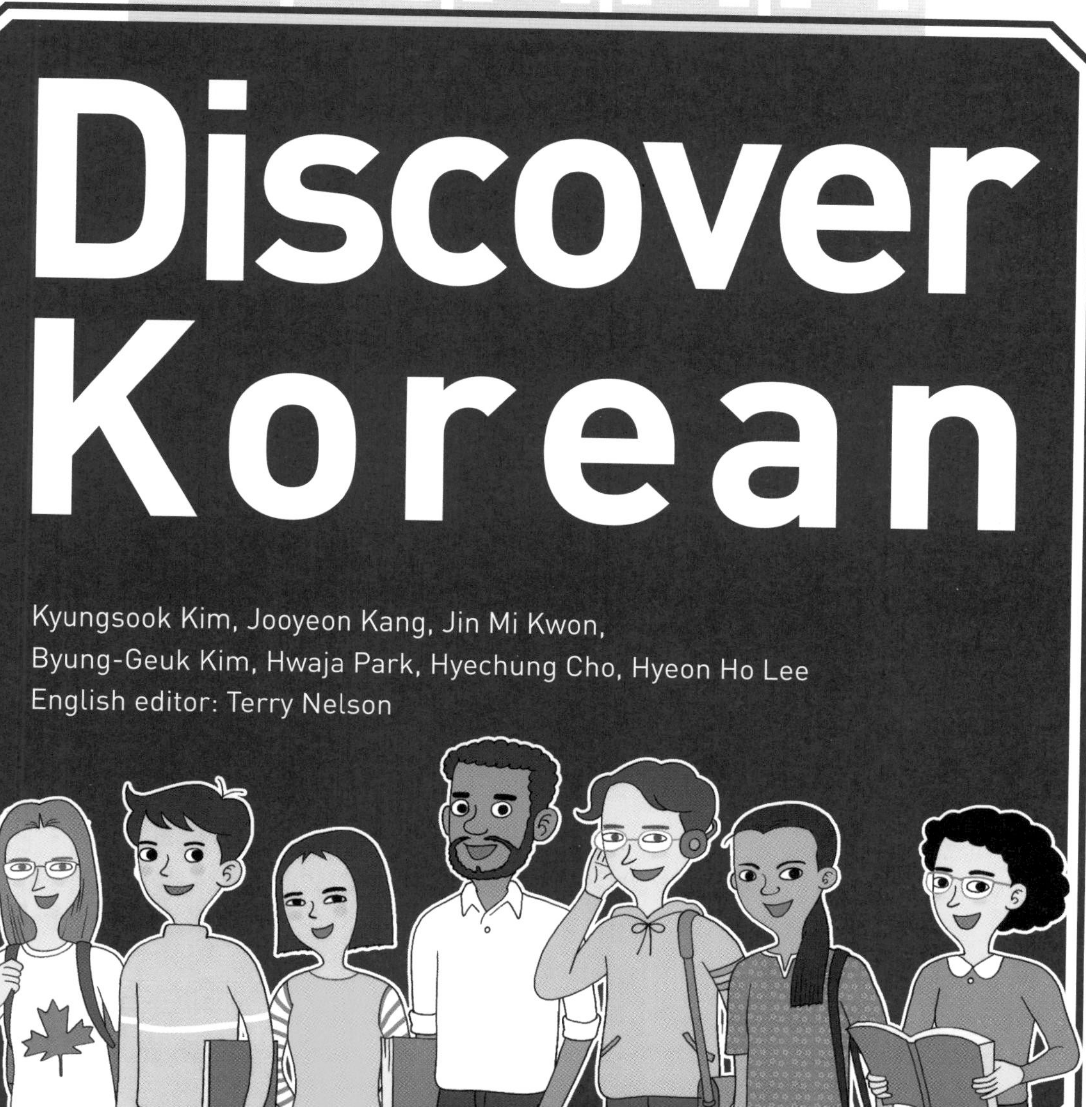

Pagijong Press Inc.

본 한국어 교과서는 현재 캐나다 앨버타 주립 대학교에서 한국어 교사로 재직하고 있는 교사들이 함께 고민하면서 만들어 낸 교재입니다. “어떻게 하면 외국인 학생들에게 한국어를 효율적으로 잘 가르칠 것인가?”에 대한 해답을 제시하기 위해 본 교재는 교수 · 학습 이론에 충실하면서 이론과 경험이 풍부한 교육 전문가의 시각에서 한국어 학습자들에게 필요한 학습 내용을 담으려고 노력했습니다. 그러므로 본 교재는 한국어 학습내용을 기존의 이론적인 시각에서 구성하는 연역적인 교재 제작 방식을 택하기 보다는 교사들이 현장에서 학습자들과 상호작용한 결과를 토대로 교재를 구성하는 귀납적인 방식을 택했습니다. 따라서 교사들이 한국어 학습내용을 수년간 학생들에게 가르쳐 본 후 학생들의 반응을 고려하면서 학습내용을 거듭하여 재구성한 방식으로서 학습자의 요구를 충실하게 반영한 현장 중심적인 교재라고 할 수 있습니다. 본 교재를 출판하게 된 구체적인 배경은 다음과 같습니다.

**첫째, 기존의 한국어 교과서들은 한국어를 배우는 학생들에게만 주로 초점이 맞추어져 있고, 정작 한국어를 가르치는 교사들에게는 적절한 안내와 교수 방법을 제시하지 못하고 있습니다.** 세계적으로 한국어 프로그램의 영역이 넓어지면서 외국에서의 한국어 교육 관련 전공자들에 대한 수요도 늘어나고 있습니다. 이들은 비록 한국어 교육 관련 전공자들이지만 아직은 한국어 교수에 익숙지 않고 경험이 적어서 많은 시간과 노력을 들여 한국어 수업을 스스로 준비해야 하는 실정입니다. 게다가 외국에서 활동하는 한국어 교사들은 대부분 고립되어 혼자 일하는 경우들이 많기 때문에 국내의 한국어 교사들에 비해서 한국어 수업을 준비하는데 상당한 시간과 노력이 요구됩니다. 이 교과서는 이러한 한국어 교사들에게 쉽게 수업을 이끌고 재미있게 한국어 수업을 운영할 수 있도록 자세한 문법 항목 설명과 그에 따른 학생들의 교실 활동, 그리고 말하기 연습을 나란히 제시하고 있어서 교사들이 쉽고 편리하게 한국어를 가르칠 수 있도록 교재를 구성하였습니다.

**둘째, 기존의 한국어 교과서들이 북미 대학교 교육 과정과 잘 맞지 않아서 한국어 교재로서의 효율도가 떨어진다는 점입니다.** 초급 단계에서 교수 시간을 일주일에 보통 4-5 시간을 기준으로 하고 있는 북미 대학교 한국어 과정에 걸맞는 한국어 교재가 필요했습니다.

**셋째, 한국어 교과서는 영어권 성인 학습자들에게는 한국어를 구조적으로 이해할 수 있도록 돕는 영어 설명과 예문이 충분히 제시되어야 합니다.** 언어를 사용하기 이전에 언어에 대한 개념을 구조적으로 이해하고 싶어하는 성인 학습자들은 늘 새로운 문법 항목을 접할때 ‘왜 그런가?’ 라는 대답을 요구하는 성향이 많습니다. 그래서 이 교과서는 이들의 구조적인 의문에 대해서 적절한 영어 설명과 예문을 제공하고 있습니다.

**넷째, 본 교과서는 교실에서 학습자들이 충분한 상호 작용을 할 수 있도록 다양한 그룹 활동이나 짝활동을 제공하고 있습니다.** 본 교과서는 한국어 수업 경험이 풍부한 교사들의 교수 자료를 바탕으로 만들어졌기 때문에 대학교에서 한국어를 배우려는 성인 학습자들에게 매우 실질적이고 재미있는 한국어 교실 활동들이 많이 제시되었다고 생각합니다. 오랜 시간의 교수 경험과 자료, 상의를 토대로 고민하면서 나온 교재이기 때문에 탈고하는데 오랜 시간이 걸렸지만 외국에서 어렵게 한국어를 가르치고 있는 많은 한국어 교사들에게 적절한 도움이 되기를 바랍니다.

2019년 5월

앨버타 대학교 한국어 프로그램 코디네이터 김경숙

공동저자 강주연, 권진미, 김병극, 박화자, 조혜정, 이현호

This book was written by instructors of the Korean language program at the University of Alberta. Together, they bring a wealth of knowledge and experience to the language teaching profession, and their insights have made this book a rich source of material for learners of Korean in a foreign language setting. One of its strengths is that it was developed inductively. It grew out of many years of reflection, dialogue and interaction between instructors, and also – importantly – between instructors and learners. This distinguishes it from other textbooks, which are developed deductively, reflecting only the instructors' point of view. The instructors who contributed to this book have gathered learners' reactions to course materials over the course of many years, and have continually revised and adapted their materials to meet the needs and expectations of those learners. This book represents the culmination of their efforts.

Another advantage of this textbook is that it provides guidelines and teaching materials for Korean instructors. This is different from most textbooks, which mainly focus on learners. As the number of Korean programs grows throughout the world, so, too, does the demand for Korean language instructors abroad. This has created a situation in which many instructors start teaching Korean abroad without appropriate teaching materials and sufficient field experience. They spend long hours preparing for class, and many develop materials alone in an isolated working environment. The time they invest in class preparation may well leave no time for program development and expansion. This textbook is intended to help. Detailed grammar explanations for both instructors and learners complement the rich variety of classroom activities and speaking exercises. Novice and experienced teachers, alike, will find the text informative and easy to use.

Another feature of this textbook is that it has a customized curriculum which fits especially well into programs in North American universities, which tend to have 4 – 5 contact hours per week at the beginning level. It also provides English explanations and examples to help learners understand the structures of grammatical concepts. Adult learners want to know 'Why?' when they encounter new grammatical expressions, and they demand specific answers. This textbook provides the answers they seek, making it an excellent resource for inquisitive adult learners.

In addition, this textbook provides plentiful opportunities for communicative interaction. It includes a rich variety of pair and group work activities, all developed by our professional Korean instructors and all designed to promote meaningful interaction.

We believe this textbook is unique in the way it integrates practice, reflection, and instructor-learner interaction. We sincerely hope it proves useful to all Korean instructors, and especially those encountering difficulties teaching outside of Korea. We hope, as well, that it proves as interesting and useful to your learners of Korean language and culture as it has to ours.

May, 2019

Kyungsook Kim Korean language program coordinator

Co-authors Jooyeon Kang, Jin Mi Kwon, Byung-Geuk Kim, Hwaja Park, Hyechung Cho, Hyeon Ho Lee

# Guidelines

Discover Korean은 영어권 지역의 대학교에서 외국어로서의 한국어를 배우려는 성인 학습자들을 위해 개발된 한국어 교재 시리즈 중 첫 번째 단계의 책이다. 따라서 이 책은 한국어에 대한 지식이 전혀 없는 성인 학습자를 대상으로 하며, 일상생활에서 필요한 가장 기본적인 수준의 말하기, 읽기, 듣기, 쓰기 능력을 향상시키기 위한 교재이다. 이 교재를 통해서 학습자들은 자기 소개 및, 사물의 성질, 장소, 시간, 숫자, 활동 등을 간단히 묘사하고 설명하는 법을 배운다. 그리고 이 교과서는 일주일에 수업 5시간, 총 14주를 기본으로 운영하는 성인 한국어 프로그램에 적절하게 맞추어져 있다.

이 교재는 총 6과로 이루어져 있으며, 각 과는 1과를 제외하고 모두 문화, 발음, 표현, 말하기, 문법, 읽기, 어휘로 구성된다. 1과에서는 본격적으로 한국어 표현들을 배우기에 앞서서 필요한 한글 철자의 발음과 읽고 쓰는 방법을 다룬다. 그리고 한글을 읽기 위해서 기본적으로 필요한 5가지 발음 규칙을 소개하고 연습한다.

**문화**는 한국어와 관련해서 한국인들의 생활에 깊숙히 스며들어 있는 한국 언어 문화를 소개한다.

**발음**에서는 실제 한국어 언어 사용에서 나타나는 기본적인 5가지 발음 규칙을 익히고, 활용하고 연습해 본다. 또한 5가지 규칙이외에도 일상생활에서 자주 쓰일 수 있는 다른 발음 규칙들도 2~6과에서 소개한다.

**표현**에서는 한국어에서 범용적으로 사용하는 관례적 표현들을 소개한다.

**말하기**는 각 과마다 3–5 개의 짧은 대화들로 구성되어 있으며 대화는 각 과에서 다루는 1–2개의 문법 항목을 활용하여 학습자들이 짧은 대화 연습을 해 볼 수 있도록 만들어졌다. 문법 항목을 소개하기 전이나 소개한 후에 대화를 연습해 볼 것을 권한다.

**문법**에서는 본문에 나오는 중요한 문법적 표현들을 소개하고, 구어적 예문을 통해 설명한다. 또한 학습자들이 각 문법적 개념을 학습한 후, 교사와의 활동, 그룹 활동, 또는 짝 활동을 하면서 그 표현들을 단계적으로 자연스럽게 익힐 수 있도록 하기 위한 말하기 활동들이 나란히 제시되어 있다.

**읽기**는 각 과를 총정리하는 지문으로서, 대화와 내레이션 두 가지로 구성되어 있으며 이해력을 돕기 위하여 관련 질문과 쓰기 공간도 제시되었다.

**어휘**에서는 이 책에서 약 210단어가 도입되었으며 새 단어는 철자 순서에 따라 각 과의 맨 뒤쪽에 정리되었다. 보충 단어는 *표를 붙이고 영어 번역을 제시하였다.

'Discover Korean' is the first book of the Korean textbook series developed for adults who wish to learn Korean in areas where English is spoken. It targets adults who have little or no previous knowledge of Korean with the objective of cultivating learners' communicative skills in speaking, listening, reading, and writing at a basic level. After studying with this textbook, learners can make simple expressions to develop ideas regarding identities, attributes, locations, time, numbers, and daily activities. In addition, this textbook is based on a curriculum which runs 5 hours per week and 14 weeks per semester for adult learners.

This textbook consists of 6 lessons. Lesson 1 deals with reading and writing the Korean alphabet, and introduces five pronunciation rules which are essential for reading Korean letters. Lessons 2 – 6 all include the following sections: culture, pronunciation, expression, speaking, grammar, reading, and vocabulary.

culture introduces some unique Korean cultural aspects which are closely related to Korean language and lifestyles.

pronunciation reviews and practices the five pronunciation rules. In lessons 2 – 6, it also introduces other pronunciation rules which Koreans often use in their daily lives.

expression introduces various idiomatic expressions which are commonly used in Korean society.

Each lesson also introduces 3 – 5 short dialogues in speaking. The purpose of these dialogues is to help learners to practice speaking short dialogues which contain 1 – 2 new grammatical expressions. This textbook recommends Korean instructors to introduce these short dialogues to learners just before studying <grammar> or right after studying <grammar>.

grammar introduces essential grammatical expressions which appear in the <speaking> and <reading> sections. These grammatical expressions are explained with colloquial examples. In addition, several speaking activities, including whole class, group work, and pair work activities, are suggested. These interactive activities enable learners to practice what they learned and to extend their practice in various ways.

reading is composed of a dialogue and a narration which synthesize what has been learned in each lesson. Questions to guide learners to an understanding of the texts, as well as space for writing, are also provided.

vocabulary introduces approximately 210 words within the 6-unit framework. New words are listed alphabetically on the last page of each lesson. Supplementary vocabulary is labeled with an *, and English translations are provided.

| Title | | Subtitles | Tasks | Grammar | Culture |
|---|---|---|---|---|---|
| 1 | 한글 | 1. Vowels | Reading and writing the vowels | | Dangun mythology |
| | | 2. Consonants | Reading and writing the consonants | | |
| | | 3. Korean Syllables | Reading and writing the Korean syllables | | |
| | | 4. Pronunciation rules | Understanding basic Korean pronunciation rules | | |
| 2 | 안녕하세요? | 1. 저는 서리나예요 | Talking about names | 은/는 (1) | Giving a bow |
| | | 2. 저도 일학년이에요 | Talking about school year and nationality | 이에요/예요<br>도 | |
| | | 3. 저는 캐나다 사람이 아니에요 | Making a negation about nationality, school year, and status | 이/가 아니에요<br>이에요/예요? | |
| | | 4. 이름이 뭐예요? | Asking and responding about names and majors | 이/가<br>은/는 vs 이/가 (1)<br>뭐예요? | |
| | | 5. 이게 뭐예요? | Asking and responding about items | 이/그/저 | |
| 3 | 어디에 있어요? | 1. 학교 식당이 어디에 있어요? | Describing the locations of items | 어디 있어요?<br>앞, 옆, 뒤, 위, 밑, 안, 밖 | Gratitude and apologies |
| | | 2. 섭 빌딩하고 토리 빌딩 안에는 뭐가 있어요? | Describing the items in a location | 에<br>뭐가 있어요?<br>하고<br>은/는 (2) | |
| | | 3. 지금 뭐 해요? | Describing daily activities | 은/는 vs 이/가 (2)<br>Verbs & Adjectives<br>-어요/아요/해요 (1)<br>뭐 해요? | |
| | | 4. 대학교가 어때요? | Describing the qualities of objects | 어때요?<br>그리고/그런데 | |

| | Title | Subtitles | Tasks | Grammar | Culture |
|---|---|---|---|---|---|
| 4 | 시간 있으세요? | 1. 오늘 시간이 있어요? | Explaining the possession of items | 이/가 있어요/없어요<br>그래서 | Address terms |
| | | 2. 누구세요? | Using honorific forms to seniors or people at a higher position | -(으)세요 (1)<br>누구 | |
| | | 3. 앉으세요 | Making a command or request | -(으)세요 (2)<br>-지 마세요 | |
| | | 4. 누가 서리나 뒤에 있어요? | Asking about a person | 누가 | |
| | | 5. 뭘 먹어요? | Making a sentence using transitive verbs | 을/를 | |
| 5 | 가족이 어떻게 돼요? | 1. 가족이 어떻게 돼요? | Discussing family members | 만<br>있으세요/계세요 | Familism and collectivism |
| | | 2. 친구하고 같이 테니스 쳐요 | Describing daily activities | -어요/아요/해요 (2)<br>하고 같이 | |
| | | 3. 커피숍에서 일해요 | Describing daily activities in a variety of places | 에, 에서 | |
| | | 4. 이거 누구의 책이에요? | Discussing people's belongings | 의<br>것/거 | |
| 6 | 지금 몇 시예요? | 1. 전화 번호가 뭐예요? | Talking about telephone numbers | Sino-Korean numbers | Koreans' handwriting of the numbers |
| | | 2. 사과 두 개 주세요 | Counting items | Native Korean numbers<br>Counters | |
| | | 3. 지금 몇 시예요? | Talking about time | Reading time | |
| | | 4. 선물 사러 백화점에 가요 | Explaining the purpose of coming or going to a place | Days of the week<br>ㄷ irregular verb<br>-(으)러 | |

Lesson

# 1

# 한글

## (Hangŭl: Korean alphabets)

Lesson 1

# 한글 (Hangŭl: Korean alphabets)

Upon completion of this lesson, you will be able to:

1. Read and write the Korean alphabet
2. Understand basic Korean pronunciation rules

**Grammatical items**

- Korean Vowels
- Korean Consonants
- Korean syllables
- Korean Pronunciation rules

## 문화(Culture)

### 'Dangun' mythology

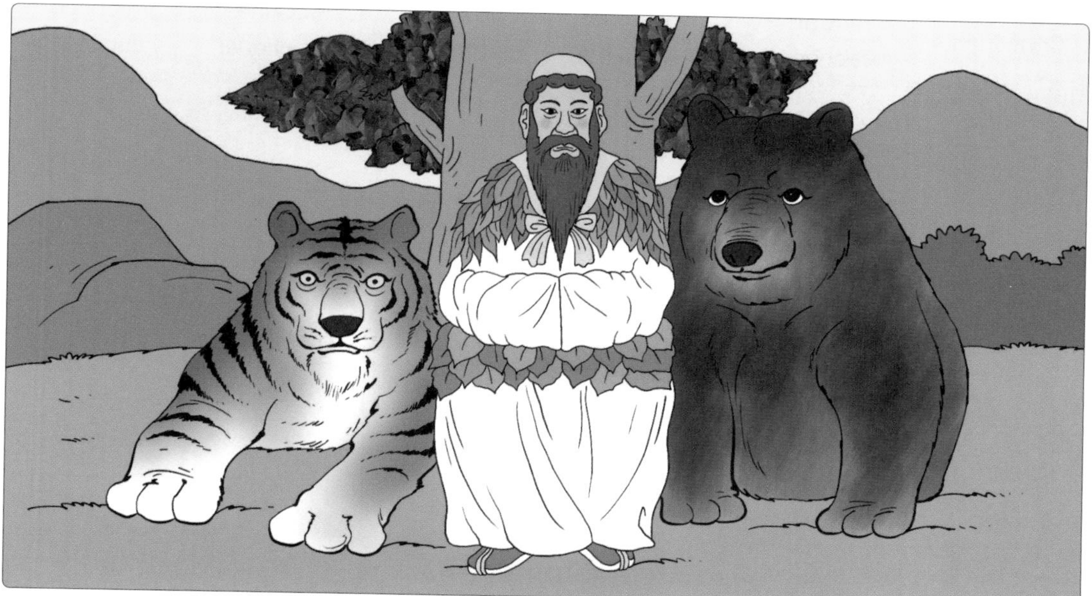

Dangun was the legendary founder of Kojosŏn, the first ever Korean kingdom in the northern part of the Korean Peninsula. He is said to be the "grandson of heaven" and "son of a bear", and to have founded the kingdom in 2333 BC. The earliest recorded version of the Dangun legend appears in the 13th-century Samguk Yusa. Dangun's ancestry legend begins with his grandfather Hwanin, the "Lord of Heaven". Hwanin had a son, Hwanung, who yearned to live on the earth among the valleys and the mountains. Hwanin permitted Hwanung and 3,000 followers to descend onto Baekdu Mountain, where Hwanung founded the Sinsi ("City of God").

A tiger and a bear prayed to Hwanung that they might become human. Upon hearing their prayers, Hwanung gave them 20 cloves of garlic and a bundle of mugwort, ordering them to eat only this sacred food and remain out of the sunlight for 100 days. The tiger gave up after about twenty days and left the cave. However, the bear persevered and was transformed into a woman. The bear-woman (Ungnyŏ) was grateful and made offerings to Hwanung. However, she lacked a husband, and soon became sad and prayed to be blessed with a child. Hwanung, moved by her prayers, took her for his wife and soon she gave birth to a son named Dangun Wanggŏm.

Dangun ascended to the throne, and built the Josŏn kingdom referred to today as Kojosŏn.

## Romanization

| Consonants | | | Vowels | | |
|---|---|---|---|---|---|
| Consonants | McCune-Reischauer | Phonetic value in IPA | Vowels/diphthongs | McCune-Reischauer | Phonetic value in IPA |
| ㅂ | b, p | [b,p] | ㅏ | a | [a] |
| ㅍ | p′ | [ph] | ㅓ | ŏ | [ə] |
| ㅃ | pp | [p′] | ㅗ | o | [o] |
| ㄷ | d, t | [d, t] | ㅜ | u | [u] |
| ㅌ | t′ | [th] | ㅐ | ae | [ɛ] |
| ㄸ | tt | [t′] | ㅔ | e | [e] |
| ㅅ | s, sh | [s, ʃ] | ㅡ | ŭ | [i] |
| ㅆ | ss | [s′, ʃ′] | ㅣ | i | [i] |
| ㅈ | j, ch | [j, c] | ㅑ | ya | [ja] |
| ㅊ | ch′ | [ch] | ㅕ | yŏ | [jə] |
| ㅉ | tch | [c′] | ㅛ | yo | [jo] |
| ㄱ | g, k | [g, k] | ㅠ | yu | [ju] |
| ㅋ | k′ | [kh] | ㅒ | yae | [jɛ] |
| ㄲ | kk | [k′] | ㅖ | ye | [je] |
| ㅁ | m | [m] | ㅘ | wa | [wa] |
| ㄴ | n | [n] | ㅙ | wae | [wɛ] |
| ㅇ | ng, Ø | [ŋ] | ㅚ | we | [Ø, we] |
| ㄹ | r, l | [r, l] | ㅝ | wŏ | [wə] |
| ㅎ | h | [h] | ㅞ | we | [we] |
| | | | ㅟ | wi | [y, wi] |
| | | | ㅢ | ŭi | [i (j), i, e] |

*Note: For your convenience, this textbook uses the 'McCune-Reischauer' transcription system.

연습 1 Let's draw the Korean national flag which is called 'Tae.gŭk.ki'.

연습 2 Draw lines to match the names and pictures of the Korean foods.

김밥 (Kim.bap) | 불고기 (Bul.go.ki) | 김치 (Kim.ch'i) | 잡채 (Jap.ch'ae) | 떡볶이 (Ttŏk.pok.i)

연습 3 If you know a famous Korean, write his/her name in the blank.

| Sports player | Actor | Actress | Singer | Others |
|---|---|---|---|---|
| | | | | |

연습 4 What else do you know about Korea? Draw things that you know about Korea, and discuss them with your classmates.

## 한글 (Hangŭl: The Korean Alphabet)

Korean is the official language of South Korea and North Korea. Korean is the 13th most widely used mother tongue in the world. Currently, 77.2 million people use Korean as their mother tongue (Korea.net, 2014).

한글 (Hangŭl) is the system of writing in Korea which was developed by King Sejong in 1443. There are 21 vowels and 19 consonants in 한글.

**8 Simple vowels**

ㅏ ㅓ ㅗ ㅜ ㅡ ㅣ ㅐ ㅔ

**13 Double vowels**

ㅑ ㅕ ㅛ ㅠ ㅒ ㅖ ㅘ ㅙ ㅚ ㅝ ㅞ ㅟ ㅢ

**14 Simple consonants**

ㄱ ㄴ ㄷ ㄹ ㅁ ㅂ ㅅ ㅇ ㅈ ㅊ ㅋ ㅌ ㅍ ㅎ

**5 Double consonants**

ㄲ ㄸ ㅃ ㅆ ㅉ

One consonant and one vowel (and sometimes one final consonant) are combined to build a syllable block. For example, the consonant of the first syllable is 'ㅂ' which produces the middle sound between [b] and [p] in English. Unlike the English [b] sound, 'ㅂ' has some aspiration, but it is less aspirated than the English [p] sound. When the consonant 'ㅂ' [b/p] is combined with the vowel 'ㅏ' [a], it makes the syllable '바' and produces the sound of [ba/pa]. One syllable, or the combination of more than one syllable, can make a word.

**An example of making a word**

ㅂ + ㅏ = 바 ('ㅂ' is pronounced as [b/p], and 'ㅏ' is pronounced as [a]) → [ba/pa]
ㄴ + ㅏ = 나 ('ㄴ' is pronounced as [n]) → [na]
ㄴ + ㅏ = 나 → [na]

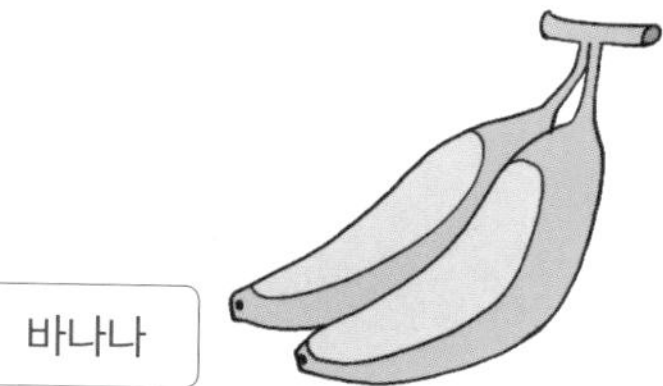

## 1. Vowels

Sounds are produced when air comes out of the lungs and vibrates the vocal cords. As shown in the picture below, the air comes from the lungs through the oral cavity or nasal cavity, and vibrates the vocal cords.

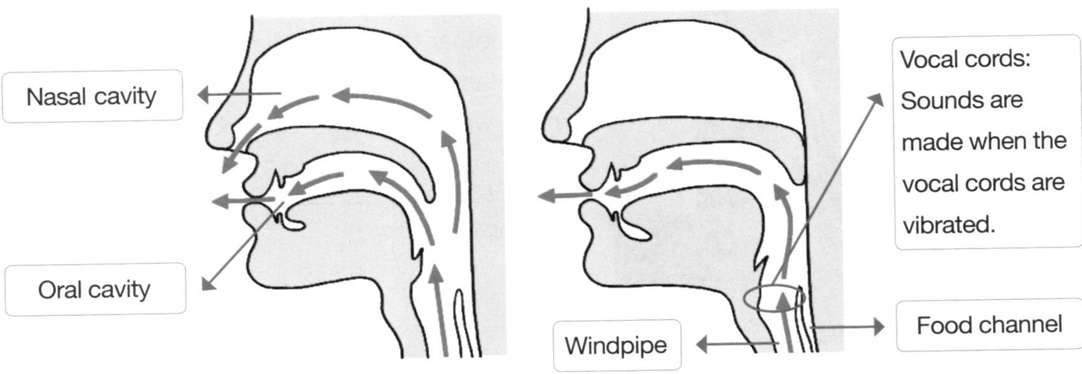


The big difference of making sounds between vowel and consonant sounds is whether the air is blocked or not. Most vowel sounds can be made without blocking the air. We can make different vowel sounds by controlling the lip shape and tongue position as long as we don't block the air. The triangle in the image below shows that different vowel sounds can be articulated according to how the lip shapes and the tongue position are controlled.

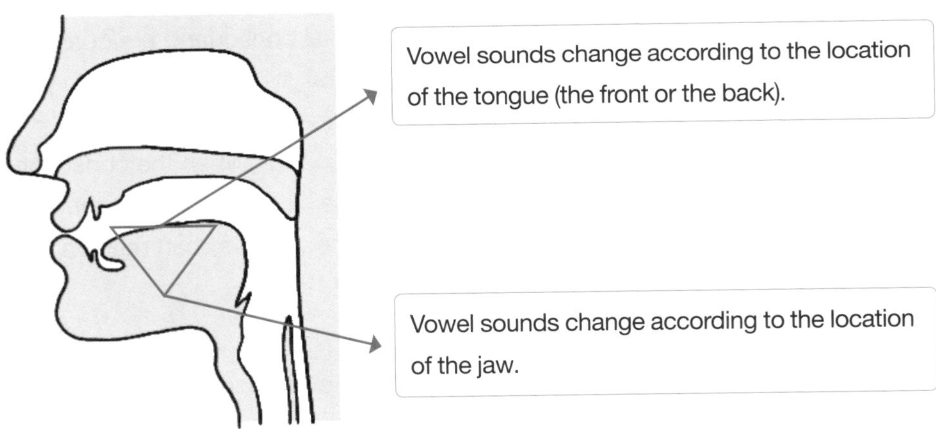

## 1-1 Simple vowels

The position of the tongue and lips change according to the sounds of vowels. The triangles below show the position of the tongue and the shape of the lip. The position of the tongue is lower when the sound is located toward the bottom, as in picture (1). For example, 'ㅏ' is produced with the tongue in the lowest position. And 'ㅣ' and 'ㅜ' are produced with the tongue in the highest position. On the other hand, as shown in picture (2), the lips get more rounded when the sound is located toward the right. In addition, the positon of the tongue also moves back to produce the right sound and moves forward to produce the left sound. For example, the shape of the lips becomes unrounded and the position of the tongue moves forward when producing 'ㅣ'. The shape of the lips becomes rounded and the position of the tongue moves back when producing 'ㅜ'.

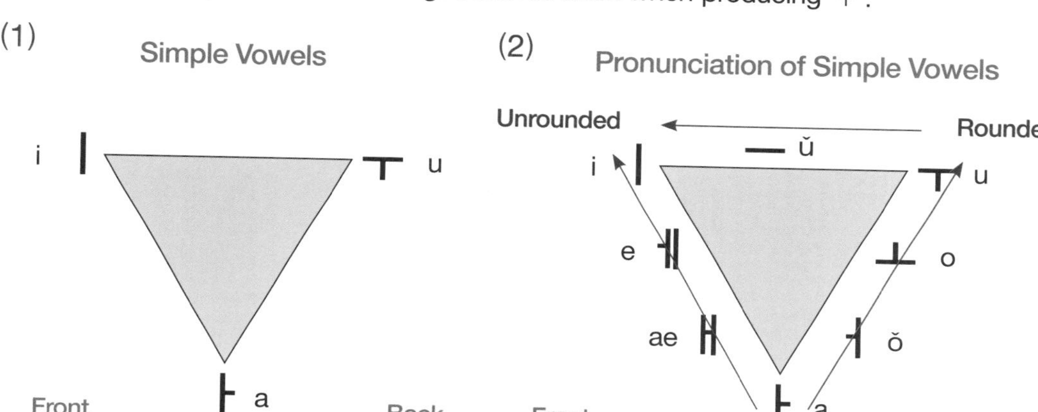


**연습 1** Listen and pronounce the following simple vowels.

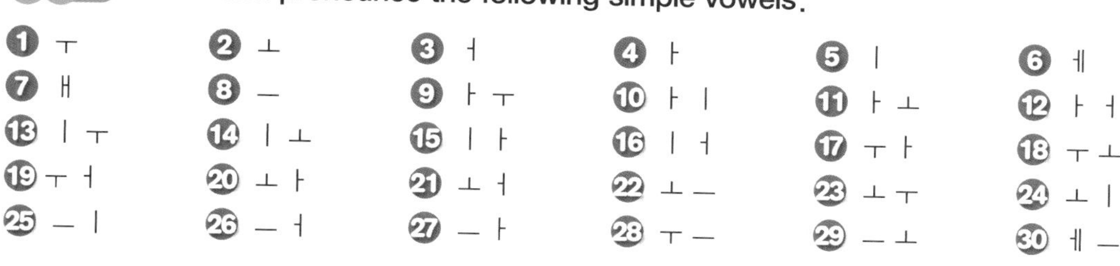

| | | | | | |
|---|---|---|---|---|---|
| ❶ ㅜ | ❷ ㅗ | ❸ ㅓ | ❹ ㅏ | ❺ ㅣ | ❻ ㅔ |
| ❼ ㅐ | ❽ ㅡ | ❾ ㅏ ㅜ | ❿ ㅏ ㅣ | ⓫ ㅏ ㅗ | ⓬ ㅏ ㅓ |
| ⓭ ㅣ ㅜ | ⓮ ㅣ ㅗ | ⓯ ㅣ ㅏ | ⓰ ㅣ ㅓ | ⓱ ㅜ ㅏ | ⓲ ㅜ ㅗ |
| ⓳ ㅜ ㅓ | ⓴ ㅗ ㅏ | 21 ㅗ ㅓ | 22 ㅗ ㅡ | 23 ㅗ ㅜ | 24 ㅗ ㅣ |
| 25 ㅡ ㅣ | 26 ㅡ ㅓ | 27 ㅡ ㅏ | 28 ㅜ ㅡ | 29 ㅡ ㅗ | 30 ㅔ ㅡ |

**연습 2** Read the following syllables. ('ㅇ' refers to no consonant sound.)

| | | | | |
|---|---|---|---|---|
| ❶ 아우 | ❷ 아이 | ❸ 아오 | ❹ 아어 | ❺ 아애 |
| ❻ 이우 | ❼ 이에 | ❽ 이오 | ❾ 이아 | ❿ 이어 |
| ⓫ 우아 | ⓬ 우오 | ⓭ 우애 | ⓮ 우이 | ⓯ 우어 |
| ⓰ 오아 | ⓱ 으어 | ⓲ 오우 | ⓳ 오애 | ⓴ 오이 |
| 21 어아 | 22 어으 | 23 어우 | 24 어오 | 25 어에 |

## 1-2 Double vowels

In Korean language, the semi-vowel sound is added to certain vowels to produce double vowel sounds. Semi-vowels have similar articulation to vowels but do not function as full vowel sounds. Rather, they function as syllable boundaries. The semi-vowel sound is shorter in duration and quickly glides into the following vowel sound. Korean language has two semi-vowels; [i] and [w]. These semi-vowels are combined with a vowel and make three different types of Korean double vowels.

1. Y-double vowel sounds are produced when [i] semi-vowel is added to certain simple vowels.'

- [i] + 'ㅏ' → 'ㅑ' [ya]
- [i] + 'ㅓ' → 'ㅕ' [yŏ]
- [i] + 'ㅗ' → 'ㅛ' [yo]
- [i] + 'ㅐ' → 'ㅒ' [yae]
- [i] + 'ㅔ' → 'ㅖ' [ye]
- [i] + 'ㅜ' → 'ㅠ' [yu]

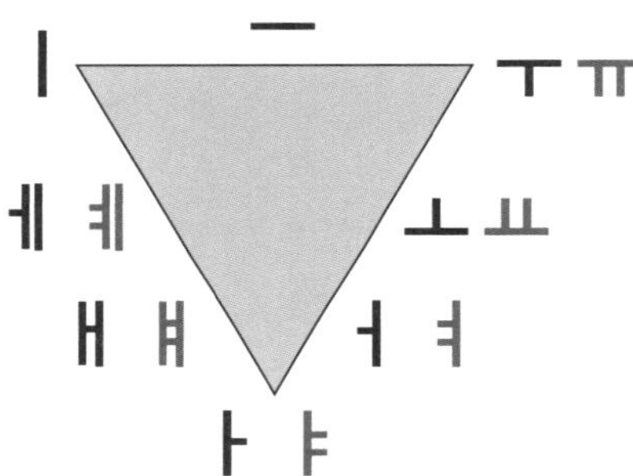


**연습 3** Listen and pronounce the following double vowels.

❶ ㅑ ❷ ㅕ ❸ ㅛ ❹ ㅠ ❺ ㅖ ❻ ㅒ

**연습 4** Pair practice:
Partner 1: Produce a random vowel sound from the list below.
Partner 2: Say the number of the sound you hear.

❶ ㅗ ❷ ㅠ ❸ ㅣ ❹ ㅕ ❺ ㅏ
❻ ㅡ ❼ ㅜ ❽ ㅑ ❾ ㅛ ❿ ㅓ

2. W-double vowel sounds are produced when [w] semi-vowel is added to certain simple vowels.

- 'ㅗ' [o] + 'ㅏ' → 'ㅘ' [wa]
- 'ㅗ' [o] + 'ㅣ' → 'ㅚ' [we]
- 'ㅜ' [u] + 'ㅔ' → 'ㅞ' [we]
- 'ㅗ' [o] + 'ㅐ' → 'ㅙ' [wae]
- 'ㅜ' [u] + 'ㅓ' → 'ㅝ' [wŏ]
- 'ㅜ' [u] + 'ㅣ' → 'ㅟ' [wi]

Note: In Korean language, 'ㅏ,' and 'ㅗ' are called 'bright vowels, and 'ㅓ' and 'ㅜ' are called dark vowels. Bright and dark vowels cannot be combined. For this reason, 'ㅏ' and 'ㅜ' cannot be combined. For the same reason, 'ㅓ' and 'ㅗ' cannot be combined.

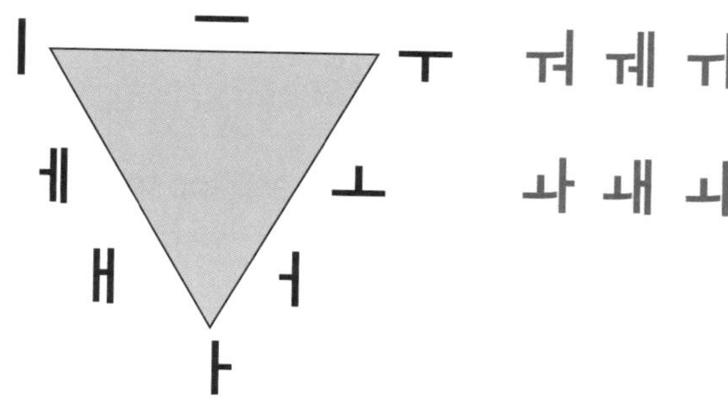


3. 'ㅣ' [i] vowel sound follows the vowel 'ㅡ' to produce a double vowel sound.

- 'ㅡ' [ŭ] + 'ㅣ' [i] → 'ㅢ' [ŭi]

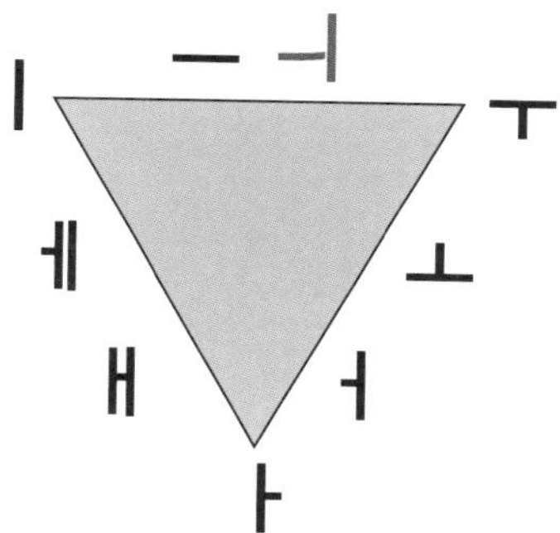


연습 5 Listen and pronounce the following vowel sounds.

1. ㅑ, ㅕ, ㅛ, ㅠ, ㅖ, ㅒ
2. ㅘ, ㅝ, ㅞ, ㅟ
3. ㅙ, ㅚ, ㅞ
4. ㅢ

**연습 6** Pair practice:
Partner 1: Randomly produce a double vowel sound from the list below
Partner 2: Say the number of the sound you hear.

| | | | | | |
|---|---|---|---|---|---|
| ① 왜 | ② 얘 | ③ 위 | ④ 워 | ⑤ 유 | ⑥ 의 |
| ⑦ 웨 | ⑧ 와 | ⑨ 요 | ⑩ 외 | ⑪ 예 | ⑫ 여 |
| ⑬ 야 | | | | | |

**연습 7** Practice the sounds of all the vowels, using the vowel cards in the online appendix.

## 1-3 How to write Korean vowels

When writing vowels, always move from left to right and top to bottom.

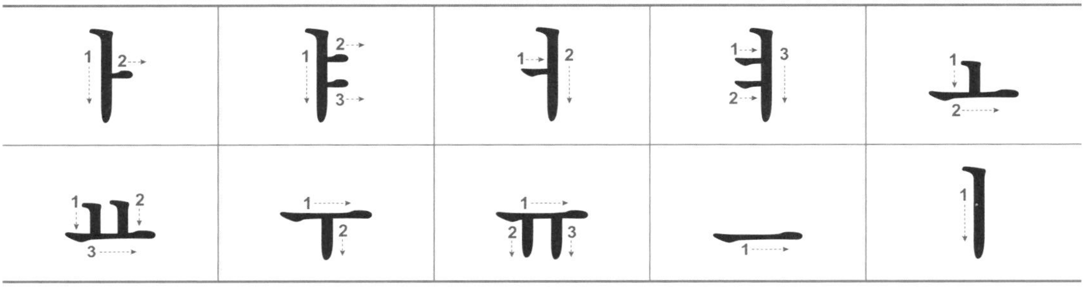

| | | | | |
|---|---|---|---|---|
| ㅏ | ㅑ | ㅓ | ㅕ | ㅗ |
| ㅛ | ㅜ | ㅠ | ㅡ | ㅣ |

## 2. Consonants

We can make different consonant sounds at five articulation points – the lips, gum ridge, hard palate, soft palate, and throat – by controlling our lips or tongue. The figure below shows a picture of all the consonant sounds.

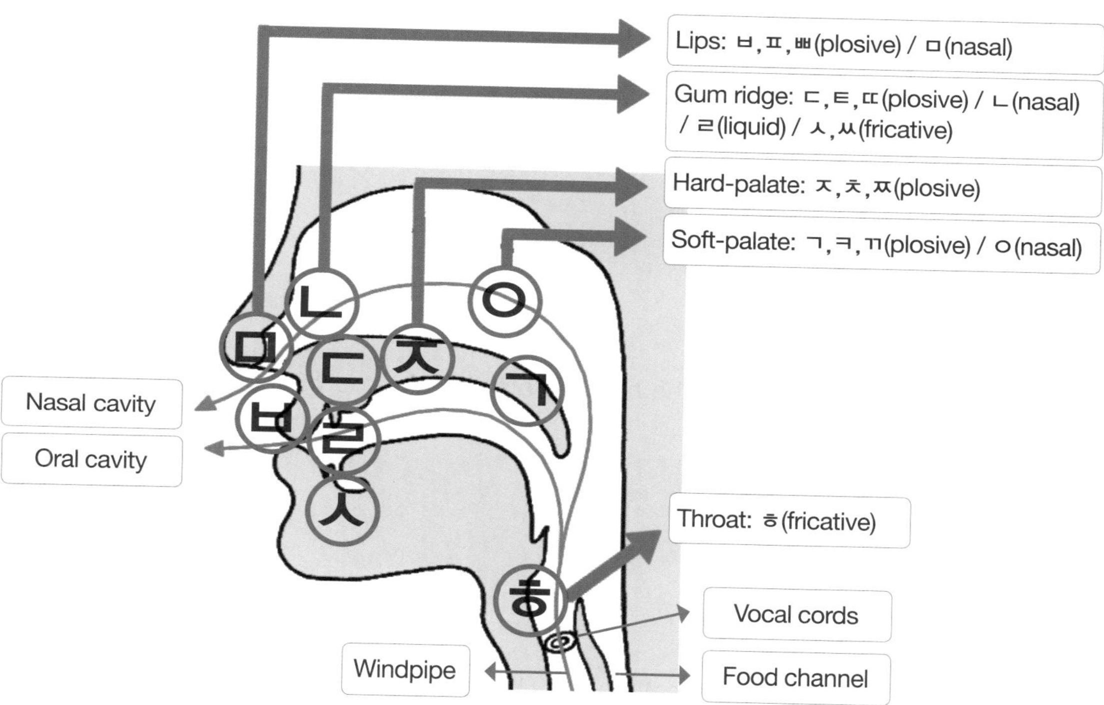


### 2-1 Making consonant sounds

Consonants are produced through the shape of the speech organs. The following speech organs produce some of the consonant sounds in particular ways.

**1.** Lip sounds

- ㅁ: Close the oral cavity with your lips so that the air goes through the nasal cavity.
- ㅂ: Block the air completely with your lips and then release it.

ㅁ [m] → ㅂ [b/p] → ㅍ [p']
→ ㅃ [pp] – tensed sound

**2.** Gum ridge sounds

- ㄴ: Close the oral cavity at the gum ridge with your tongue so that the air goes through the nasal cavity.
- ㄷ: Block the air completely at the gum ridge with your tongue and then release it.
- ㄹ (light L): Lightly touch the gum ridge with your tongue tip–달
- ㄹ (flat R): Don't roll your tongue too much–라디오

ㄴ [n] → ㄷ [d/t] → ㅌ [t']
→ ㄸ [tt] – tensed sound
→ ㄹ [r /l]

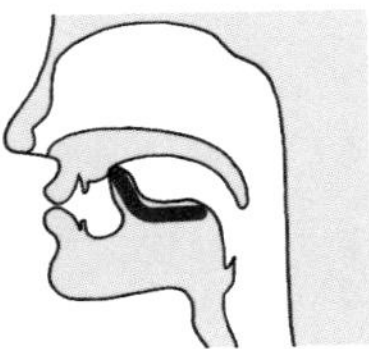

- ㅅ: Block the air partially at the gum ridge to make hissing sounds

ㅅ [s] → ㅆ [ss] – tensed sound

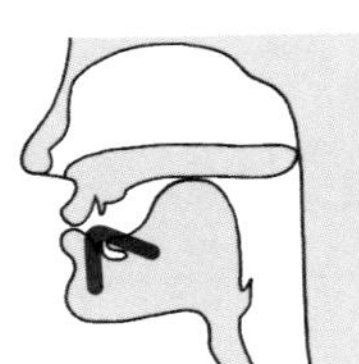

**3.** Hard–palate sounds

- ㅈ: Block the air completely at the hard–palate with the top of your tongue and then release it.

ㅈ [ch/j] → ㅊ [ch']
→ ㅉ [tch] – tensed sound

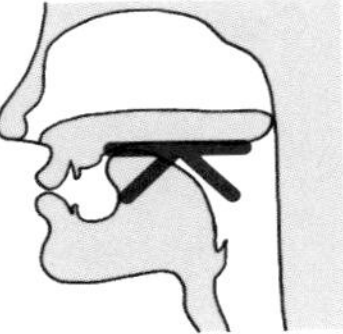

**4.** Soft–palate (velar) sounds

- ㅇ: Close your oral cavity at the soft palate with your soft palate tip so that the air goes through the nasal cavity.
- ㄱ: Block the air completely at the soft palate with your tongue back and then release it.

ㄱ [g/k] → ㅋ [k']
→ ㄲ [kk] – tensed sound

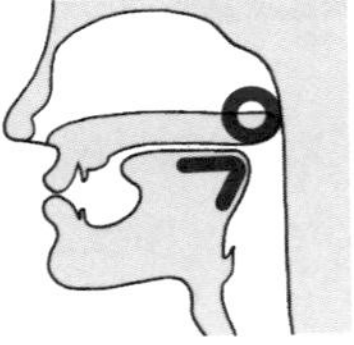

**5.** Throat sounds

Block the air partially at the throat so that the air escapes through a small opening in the oral cavity.

ㅎ [h]

Tables of all consonants

| Plain | ㄱ | ㄴ | ㄷ | ㄹ | ㅁ | ㅂ | ㅅ | ㅇ | ㅈ |
|---|---|---|---|---|---|---|---|---|---|
| Aspirated | ㅋ | | ㅌ | | | ㅍ | | ㅎ | ㅊ |
| Tensed | ㄲ | | ㄸ | | | ㅃ | ㅆ | | ㅉ |

연습 1 Listen and pronounce the following consonant sounds.

1. ㄱ, ㄴ, ㄷ, ㄹ, ㅁ, ㅂ, ㅅ, ㅇ, ㅈ, ㅊ, ㅋ, ㅌ, ㅍ, ㅎ
2. ㄱ, ㄷ, ㅂ, ㅅ, ㅈ
3. ㄲ, ㄸ, ㅃ, ㅆ, ㅉ
4. ㅋ, ㅌ, ㅍ, ㅊ

연습 2 Pair practice:

Partner 1: Produce a random consonant sound from the list below.

Partner 2: Say the number of the sound you hear.

1. ㅊ
2. ㄷ
3. ㅆ
4. ㅁ
5. ㅂ
6. ㅅ
7. ㅃ
8. ㄲ
9. ㅇ
10. ㄸ
11. ㅈ
12. ㅋ
13. ㅌ
14. ㅉ
15. ㄱ
16. ㅍ
17. ㄹ
18. ㅎ
19. ㄴ

연습 3 Practice the sounds of all the consonants, using the consonant cards in the online appendix.

## 2-2 How to write Korean consonants

When writing consonants, the writing principle of moving from left to right and top to bottom is still kept.

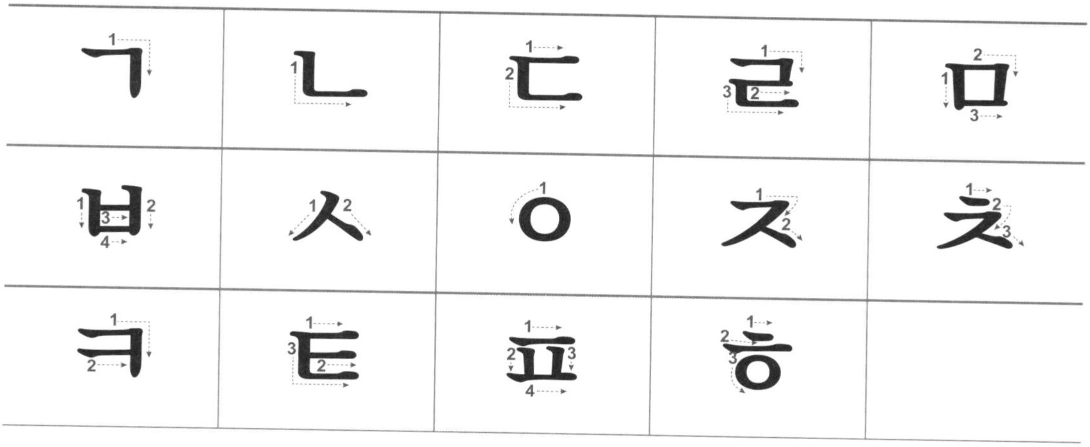

| ㄱ | ㄴ | ㄷ | ㄹ | ㅁ |
|---|---|---|---|---|
| ㅂ | ㅅ | ㅇ | ㅈ | ㅊ |
| ㅋ | ㅌ | ㅍ | ㅎ | |

## 3. Korean syllables

Korean syllables always begin with an initial consonant. Then a vowel is placed on the right or on the bottom of the consonant. The syllable construction can stop with a consonant and a vowel, or it can have one more consonant on the bottom. The second consonant is called 'final consonant (Bach'im),' because it is the last sound in a syllable.

### 3-1 Korean syllables without a final consonant (Bach'im)

Many Korean syllables are composed of one consonant and one vowel. The combination of one consonant and one vowel follows three different styles as shown below. When you read a syllable, sound out the initial consonant and then the following vowel.
(Note: C: Consonant, V: Vowel)

**1.** One consonant + One of the vertical vowels (ㅏ, ㅑ, ㅓ, ㅕ, ㅣ, ㅐ, ㅔ, ㅒ, ㅖ)

| ㄱ + ㅏ | 가 | ㅁ + ㅑ | 먀 |
|---|---|---|---|
| ㄴ + ㅓ | 너 | ㅂ + ㅕ | 벼 |
| ㄷ + ㅣ | 디 | ㄸ + ㅐ | 때 |
| ㄹ + ㅔ | 레 | ㅇ + ㅒ | 얘 |

**2.** One consonant + One of the horizontal vowels (ㅗ, ㅛ, ㅜ, ㅠ, ㅡ)

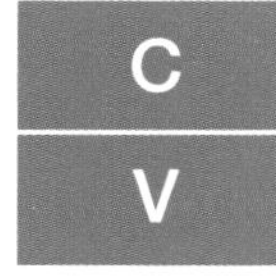


| ㄱ + ㅗ | 고 | ㅁ + ㅛ | 묘 |
|---|---|---|---|
| ㄴ + ㅜ | 누 | ㅂ + ㅠ | 뷰 |
| ㄷ + ㅡ | 드 | ㄲ + ㅗ | 꼬 |

**3.** One consonant + One of the following double vowels (ㅘ, ㅙ, ㅚ, ㅝ, ㅞ, ㅟ, ㅢ)

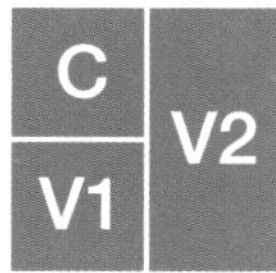


| ㄱ + ㅞ | 궤 | ㅁ + ㅝ | 뭐 |
|---|---|---|---|
| ㄴ + ㅙ | 놰 | ㅈ + ㅟ | 쥐 |
| ㄷ + ㅚ | 되 | ㅎ + ㅢ | 희 |

**연습 1** Listen and pronounce the following syllables.

| | | | | | | | | |
|---|---|---|---|---|---|---|---|---|
| ① 가 | 나 | 다 | 라 | | ② 거 | 너 | 더 | 러 |
| ③ 고 | 노 | 도 | 로 | | ④ 구 | 누 | 두 | 루 |
| ⑤ 그 | 느 | 드 | 르 | | ⑥ 기 | 니 | 디 | 리 |

연습 2 Listen and pronounce the following syllables.

| | | | | | | | | | |
|---|---|---|---|---|---|---|---|---|---|
| ❶ 마 | 미 | 무 | 메 | 모 | ❷ 바 | 비 | 부 | 베 | 보 |
| ❸ 나 | 니 | 두 | 데 | 도 | ❹ 라 | 리 | 수 | 세 | 소 |
| ❺ 파 | 피 | 추 | 체 | 초 | ❻ 카 | 키 | 후 | 헤 | 호 |

연습 3 Listen and pronounce the following syllables.

| | | | | | | | | | |
|---|---|---|---|---|---|---|---|---|---|
| ❶ 가 | 나 | 다 | 라 | 마 | ❷ 보 | 소 | 오 | 조 | 초 |
| ❸ 구 | 누 | 두 | 루 | 무 | ❹ 케 | 테 | 페 | 헤 | 베 |
| ❺ 그 | 느 | 드 | 르 | 므 | ❻ 봐 | 줘 | 쉬 | 웨 | 괘 |

연습 4 Make your own syllables and then read them.

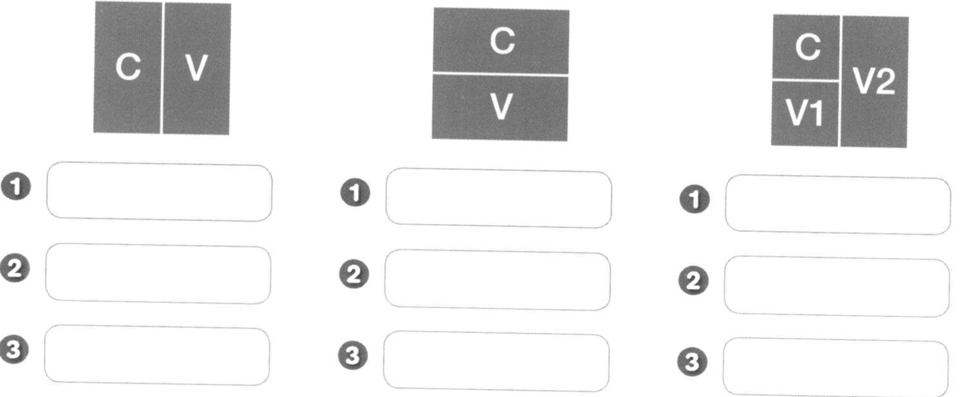


연습 5 Practice reading the words on the cards in the online appendix, which include syllables without final consonants.

## 3-2 How to make a syllable with a final consonant (Bach'im)

Some Korean syllables are combined with three phonetic sounds; the first consonant, a vowel, and a second consonant. The three different combination styles are shown below. Sound out the initial consonant and the following vowel, making them flow into the final consonant.

(Note: C: Consonant, V: Vowel, C(C): Final consonant)

1. One consonant + One of the following vowels (ㅏ, ㅑ, ㅓ, ㅕ, ㅣ, ㅔ, ㅐ, ㅖ, ㅒ) + Final consonant

C V / C(C)

| One consonant + One vowel | Final | Syllable |
|---|---|---|
| ㅅ + ㅏ | ㄴ | 산 |
| ㄱ + ㅣ | ㄹ | 길 |

2. One consonant + One of the following vowels (ㅗ, ㅛ, ㅜ, ㅠ, ㅡ) + Final consonant

C / V / C(C)

| One consonant + One vowel | Final | Syllable |
|---|---|---|
| ㄴ + ㅜ | ㄴ | 눈 |
| ㅁ + ㅗ | ㅁ | 몸 |

3. One consonant + One of the following vowels (ㅘ, ㅙ, ㅚ, ㅝ, ㅞ, ㅟ, ㅢ) + Final consonant

C / V1 / V2 / C(C)

| One consonant + One vowel | Final | Syllable |
|---|---|---|
| ㄷ + ㅚ | ㄴ | 된 |
| ㄱ + ㅝ | ㄱ | 권 |

**연습 6** **Make your own syllables and then read them.**

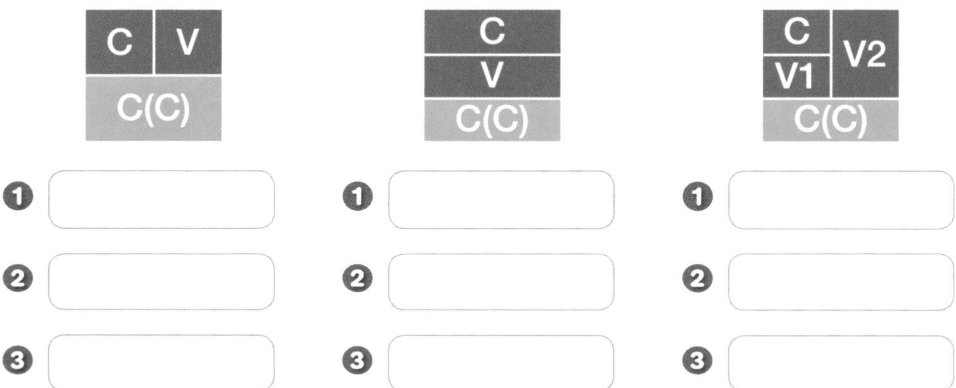


(Note: In the final consonant position, one or two double consonants may occur. The following combinations of double consonants are available in the final consonant position.)

| ㄲ | ㅆ | ㄳ | ㄵ | ㄶ | ㄺ | ㄻ | ㄼ | ㄽ | ㄾ | ㄿ | ㅀ | ㅄ |
|---|---|---|---|---|---|---|---|---|---|---|---|---|

1. 흙을 밟아요. 2. 책을 읽어요. 3. 값이 싸요. 4. 의자에 앉아요.
5. 아름다운 삶 6. 시를 읊어요

## 3-3 Pronunciations of Final Consonants

The consonants sound differently when they are used as finals (the last consonant). Each final consonant is pronounced only in one of 7 different ways (ㄱ, ㄴ, ㄷ, ㄹ, ㅁ, ㅂ, ㅇ).

**1.** Voiced finals

| | | | |
|---|---|---|---|
| Nasal finals | ㄴ | [n] in 'sun' | 돈, 반찬 |
| | ㅁ | [m] in 'term' | 곰, 사람 |
| | ㅇ | [ng] in 'going' | 강아지, 공주 |
| Liquid final | ㄹ | [l] in 'pool' | 물, 길, 할머니 |

**2.** Voiceless finals

| Final | Non-nasal finals | Examples |
|---|---|---|
| ㄱ, ㅋ, ㄲ | [k'] in 'sick' without releasing the sound | 한국, 부엌 |
| ㄷ, ㅅ, ㅈ, ㅊ, ㅌ, ㅎ | [t'] in 'cat' without releasing the sound | 닫다, 옷, 짖다, 꽃, 끝, 낳다 |
| ㅂ, ㅍ | [p'] in 'pop' without releasing the sound | 밥, 잎 |

**연습 7** **Indicate the final sound of each syllable by its representing sound (ㄱ, ㄷ, or ㅂ) as in the example.**

(Example: 갓 → [ㄷ])

❶ 각 ❷ 간 ❸ 갇 ❹ 갈 ❺ 감 ❻ 갑
❼ 갓 ❽ 갖 ❾ 강 ❿ 갖 ⓫ 각 ⓬ 같
⓭ 갚 ⓮ 갛

**연습 8** **Read the following syllables.**

❶ 각, 낙, 닥, 락, 막, 박, 삭
❷ 앗, 잣, 찻, 캇, 탓, 팟, 핫
❸ 갑, 납, 답, 랍, 맙, 밥, 삽
❹ 앙, 장, 창, 캉, 탕, 팡, 항
❺ 감, 남, 담, 람, 맘, 밤, 삼
❻ 안, 잔, 찬, 칸, 탄, 판, 한
❼ 갈, 날, 달, 랄, 말, 발, 살

**연습 9** **Read the following syllables.**

❶ 정, 전 ❷ 넌, 넝 ❸ 던, 덩 ❹ 간, 강 ❺ 만, 망
❻ 반, 방 ❼ 공, 곰 ❽ 송, 솜 ❾ 옹, 옴 ❿ 종, 좀
⓫ * 소리, 다리, 무리 ⓬ ** 솔, 달, 물

* When ㄹ comes between vowels; don't let your tongue touch your gum ridge.
– 소리, 다리, 무리 (Flap *r*)

** When ㄹ comes in the end of a word; make your tongue touch your gum ridge.
– 솔, 달, 물 (Light *l*)

**연습 10** Read the following words.

| | | | | |
|---|---|---|---|---|
| ① 바나나 | ② 토마토 | ③ 캐나다 | ④ 오렌지 | ⑤ 아이스크림 |
| ⑥ 피자 | ⑦ 케이크 | ⑧ 마우스 | ⑨ 커피 | ⑩ 버스 |
| ⑪ 주스 | ⑫ 스키 | ⑬ 스케이트 | ⑭ 햄버거 | ⑮ 파티 |

**연습 11** Read the following names.

| | | |
|---|---|---|
| ① 브리트니 스피어스 | ② 잭키 찬 | ③ 저스틴 비버 |
| ④ 마이클 잭슨 | ⑤ 데이비드 베컴 | ⑥ 슈렉 |

**연습 12** Practice reading the Korean words on the cards in the online appendix which show the syllables with final consonants.

## 3-4 Writing English names in Korean

Korean syllables are usually composed of one consonant, one vowel, and one final consonant (optional). According to this rule, English sounds can be broken into blocks to make a Korean syllable. When the block does not have a vowel sound after a consonant sound, the vowel '—' is added to the consonant to make a syllable block.

| Names | Sounds | Korean alphabets of the sound | Korean syllables |
|---|---|---|---|
| Britney | [b – ri – t'– ni] | ㅂ – ㄹㅣ – ㅌ – ㄴㅣ | 브리트니 |
| Justin | [jŏ – s – t'in] | ㅈㅓ – ㅅ – ㅌㅣ – ㄴ | 저스틴 |
| Michael | [ma – i – k'l] | ㅁㅏ – ㅣ – ㅋ – ㄹ | 마이클 |
| David | [de – i – vi – d] | ㄷㅔ – ㅣ – ㅂㅣ – ㄷ | 데이비드 |

**연습 13** Write your name in Korean, and introduce yourself to your classmates, as suggested in the example.

| English spelling of your first name | pronunciation | Korean |
|---|---|---|
| (Example) Jennifer | Je – ni – fŏ | 제니퍼 |
| | | |

(Example of self-introduction)

안녕하세요. 저는 [          ] 입니다.

Hello. I am (Korean name).

## 3-5 Names of the consonants

| ㄱ | 기역 | ㄴ | 니은 | ㄷ | 디귿 | ㄹ | 리을 | ㅁ | 미음 | ㅂ | 비읍 |
|---|---|---|---|---|---|---|---|---|---|---|---|
| ㅅ | 시옷 | ㅇ | 이응 | ㅈ | 지읒 | ㅊ | 치읓 | ㅋ | 키읔 | ㅌ | 티읕 |
| ㅍ | 피읖 | ㅎ | 히읗 | | | | | | | | |
| ㄲ | 쌍기역 | ㄸ | 쌍디귿 | ㅃ | 쌍비읍 | ㅆ | 쌍시옷 | ㅉ | 쌍지읒 | | |

The name of each consonant letter begins and ends with the consonant, as shown in the following example. And five of the Korean consonants have twin counterparts, known as '쌍 [ssang],' and they are used to represent the tenseness.

ㄴ : 니 + 은

**연습 14** Pair practice:
Partner 1 : Say the name of a random consonant.
Partner 2 : Write the consonant you hear.

1
2
3
4
5
6
7
8
9

**연습 15** Listen to the names of the consonants and write them in the blanks.

1
2
3
4
5
6
7
8
9

## 4. Pronunciation rules

Korean words are not always pronounced as they are written because of the difficulty in pronouncing the syllable together. In order to make the words easy to pronounce, it is necessary to understand some Korean pronunciation rules. Here, in this lesson, only the 5 main pronunciation rules will be introduced. There are a few more pronunciation rules, as well as exceptions, but they will be introduced in later lessons.

### 4-1 Syllable-final closure

When the final consonant of a syllable has the voiceless sound, such as ㄱ, ㅋ, ㄲ, ㄷ, ㅌ, ㄸ, ㅂ, ㅍ, ㅅ, ㅆ, ㅈ, ㅊ, ㅎ they are unleased, and are produced as one of three representative sounds; [ㄱ], [ㅂ], ㅎ, they are unleased, [ㄷ].

| Finals | Unreleased final sounds | Examples |
|---|---|---|
| ㄱ, ㅋ, ㄲ | [ㄱ] | 조각, 부엌 |
| ㅂ, ㅍ | [ㅂ] | 밥, 잎, 서랍 |
| ㄷ, ㅌ, ㅅ, ㅆ, ㅈ, ㅊ, ㅎ | [ㄷ] | 곳, 빛, 빗, 솥, 맛, 꽃 |

연습 1 **Write the following words as they sound as in the example.**

(Example: 옷 [옫])

1. 잎
2. 곳
3. 맛
4. 빛
5. 꽃
6. 바닥
7. 기역
8. 서랍
9. 부엌

### 4-2 Re-syllabification

When the first consonant of the following syllable is [ㅇ] (zero sound), it is replaced by the final consonant of the previous syllable. When the initial syllable has a double final, the first consonant of the double final usually stays and the second consonant of the double final is carried over to the next syllable. However, when the double final has the same double consonants such as ㄲ or ㅆ, they are carried over together to the next syllable, as shown below.

- 책이 → [채기]
- 갔어요 → [가써요]
- 앉으세요 → [안즈세요]

연습 2 Write the following words as they sound.

1. 연필을
2. 먹었어요
3. 창문이
4. 있어요
5. 가을에
6. 앞으로
7. 들으세요
8. 집에서
9. 꽃이
10. 앉으세요
11. 읽어요
12. 팔아서
13. 틈틈이
14. 잠옷
15. 받았어요
16. 할아버지
17. 낮에
18. 넓어요
19. 닦아요
20. 벤이 집에서 잠을 자고 있어요

## 4-3 Tensification

When the first consonant of the following syllable (except 'ㅇ') bumps into [ㄱ], [ㄷ], [ㅂ] of the previous syllable, it becomes its tensed sound. However, this tensification occurs only when the first consonant of the following syllable has the corresponding tensed sound such as [ㄲ], [ㄸ], [ㅃ], [ㅆ], or [ㅉ].

- 숙제 → [숙쩨]
- 먹방 → [먹빵]
- 책상 → [책쌍]

연습 3 Write the following words as they sound.

1. 같지요
2. 깍두기
3. 부엌도
4. 색시

Lesson 1 Lesson 2 Lesson 3 Lesson 4 Lesson 5 Lesson 6

⑤ 갔다 ☐　　⑥ 밥과 ☐

⑦ 낚다가 ☐　　⑧ 몇 살 ☐

⑨ 식당 ☐　　⑩ 약국 ☐

⑪ 닫다 ☐　　⑫ 학교 ☐

⑬ 약국에 갔더니 약사가 있었다 ☐

## 4-4 Nasalization

[ㄱ], [ㄷ], [ㅂ] final sounds become their corresponding nasal consonants, when the first consonant of the following syllable has nasal sounds, such as [ㄴ] or [ㅁ].

| Unreleased final sounds | Nasal sounds | Examples |
| --- | --- | --- |
| ㄱ, ㅋ, ㄲ → | [ㅇ] | 일학년 → [일항년] |
| ㅂ, ㅍ → | [ㅁ] | 반갑습니다 → [반갑씀니다] |
| ㄷ, ㅌ, ㅅ, ㅆ, ㅈ, ㅊ, ㅎ → | [ㄴ] | 끝나다 → [끈나다] |

Note: The nasalization occurs in the same location of the particular sound organ, for the convenience of making sounds. For example, [ㅂ] is changed into [ㅁ] because they are produced by the same sound organ (lips). In the same way, [ㄱ] is changed into [ㅇ] because they are both soft-palate sounds. [ㄷ] is changed into [ㄴ] because they are both gum-ridge sounds.

**연습 4** Write the following words as they sound.

① 일학년 ☐　　② 이학년 ☐

③ 삼학년 ☐　　④ 사학년 ☐

⑤ 반갑습니다 ☐　　⑥ 고맙습니다 ☐

## 4-5 Double consonant reduction

Korean has several types of double consonant finals (ㄲ, ㅆ, ㄳ, ㄵ, ㄶ, ㄺ, ㄻ, ㄼ, ㄽ, ㄾ, ㄿ, ㅀ, ㅄ). However, these double consonants are pronounced only as one consonant sound. The double final consonant usually produces only the sound of the consonant which is placed on the left side, but there are some exceptions. For example, 'ㄺ' is pronounced as [ㄱ] when the following syllable has the first consonant sound. (Note: ㄺ, ㄻ, or ㄿ produce the sound of the consonant which is placed on the right side.) However, when the first consonant of the following syllable has a zero sound, 'ㄺ' is also split for the carry-over. [ㄹ] remains as the final of the previous syllable and [ㄱ] is carried over to the next syllable.

• 여덟 → [여덜]  • 값 → [갑]  • 없다 → [업따]  • 읽다 → [익따]  • 읽어요 → [일거요]

연습 5 Write the following words as they sound.

1. 여덟
2. 앉다
3. 많소
4. 넓다
5. 넓어요
6. 닭
7. 읽다
8. 읽어요
9. 맑다
10. 맑아요
11. 짧다
12. 짧아요

Lesson 1 Lesson 2 Lesson 3 Lesson 4 Lesson 5 Lesson 6

Lesson

# 2

# 안녕하세요?

(Hello!)

Lesson 2

# 안녕하세요? (Hello!)

말하기 1 저는 서리나예요. (I am Cerina.)

말하기 2 저도 1학년이에요. (I am also a first-year student.)

말하기 3 저는 캐나다 사람이 아니에요. (I am not Canadian.)

말하기 4 이름이 뭐예요? (What's your name?)

말하기 5 이게 뭐예요? (What's this?)

Upon completion of this lesson, you will be able to:

1. Ask and respond to questions about names, nationality, school year, status, jobs, and major
2. Ask and respond to questions about the names of objects

**Grammatical items**

- N1은/는 N2이에요 (N1 is N2.)
- 도 (Particle – also)
- N1은/는 N2이/가 아니에요. (N1 isn't N2.)
- 이에요/예요? (Making a question)
- 이/가 (Subject particle)
- 이게/그게/저게 뭐예요? (What is this/that?)

## 문화 (Culture) Giving a bow

Koreans bow differently, according to the situation.

| Light bow | Ordinary bow | Deep bow | Big bow |
|---|---|---|---|
| A light bow is usually made to casual acquaintances, such as classmates, alumni, co-workers, or neighours. | An ordinary bow is made to seniors, such as teachers, boss, or older people. | A deep bow is made in formal situations like a speech. These situations also require formal style language: 안녕하십니까? | Another kind of deep bow is made on special holidays to parents, grandparents, and ancestors. |

## 발음 (Pronunciations) Review

**1.** Final 'ㅂ' is nasalized because of a neighboring nasal consonant.

반갑습니다 [ ] 학생입니다 [ ]

**2.** Final 'ㄱ' is nasalized into 'ㅇ' because of a neighboring nasal consonant.

일학년 [ ] 이학년 [ ]

**3.** When subsequent syllables do not have a consonant sound, the previous final is pronounced as the first consonant sound.

선생님은 [ ] 한국어 [ ] 사람이에요 [ ]

## 표현 (Expression) 안녕하세요?

**선생님** 안녕하세요? 서리나.

**서리나** 안녕하세요? 선생님.

**선생님** 반가워요.

| | |
|---|---|
| **안녕하세요?** | Hello, Hi. This expression can be used at any time of the day.<br>The appropriate response would be '안녕하세요?' |
| **반가워요.** | Glad to meet you. |

**연습**

Greet each other with your partner.

A 안녕하세요? (Name)____________________.

B 안녕하세요? (Name)____________________.

A 반가워요.

## 말하기 (Speaking) 1. 안녕하세요?

서리나 안녕하세요? 저는 서리나예요.

벤 안녕하세요? 저는 벤이에요.

서리나 반가워요.

Cerina Hello. I'm Cerina.

Ben Hello. I'm Ben.

Cerina Glad to meet you.

## 문법 (Grammar) 1

### 1-1 Basic Korean sentence structure

One of the basic Korean sentence structures is predicated using a copular verb*. This sentence structure is useful to introduce a person or an object. Korean sentence structure is different from that of English. It follows a Subject, Complement, Verb order as shown in the table below.

| | | | |
|---|---|---|---|
| English | Topic | Copular-verb | Complement |
| | I | am | Korean |
| Korean | Topic + Particle | Complement | Copular-verb |
| | 저는** (I) | 한국사람 (Korean) | 이에요 (am) |

*Copular verb is a verb that links a subject to a complement that refers to the subject.
**'저' is the humble form of '나'. '저' can be used when you want to be polite to the listener.

### 1-2 Topic particle '은/는'

The topic particle '은/는' is attached to the end of a noun to make it the topic of a sentence.
(1) 벤은* 학생이에요. (Ben is a student.)
 *Topic particle '은' is attached when the noun ends in a consonant.
(2) 서리나는* 캐나다 사람이에요. (Cerina is a Canadian.)
 *Topic particle '는' is attached when the noun ends in a vowel.

**연습 1** Write 은 or 는 after each name.

| | | | | | |
|---|---|---|---|---|---|
| | | | | | |
| 줄리아 | 준 | 리아 | 샤닐 | 제니 | 선생님 |

**연습 2** Write your first name in Korean, and write the proper topic particle after your first name.

Name: ______ ______
Your first name Topic particle

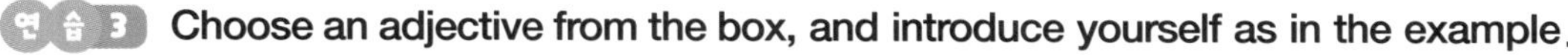

**연습 3 Choose an adjective from the box, and introduce yourself as in the example.**

| | | | |
|---|---|---|---|
| 예뻐요 (pretty) | 잘 생겼어요 (handsome) | 귀여워요 (cute) | 착해요 (nice) |
| 친절해요 (kind) | 부지런해요 (diligent) | 용감해요 (brave) | 명랑해요 (cheerful) |
| 똑똑해요 (smart) | 사교적이에요 (social) | 적극적이에요 (active) | 조용해요 (quiet) |

(Example) 안녕하세요. 저는 서리나입니다*. 저는 부지런해요. (*입니다: to be)
(Hello. I am Cerina. I am diligent.)

**연습 4 Choose an adjective from the above, and introduce your friend to your group as in the example.**

(Example) 친구*서리나입니다. 서리나는 예뻐요. (*친구:friend)
(This is my friend, Cerina. She is pretty.)

## 말하기 (Speaking) 2. 저는 1학년이에요.

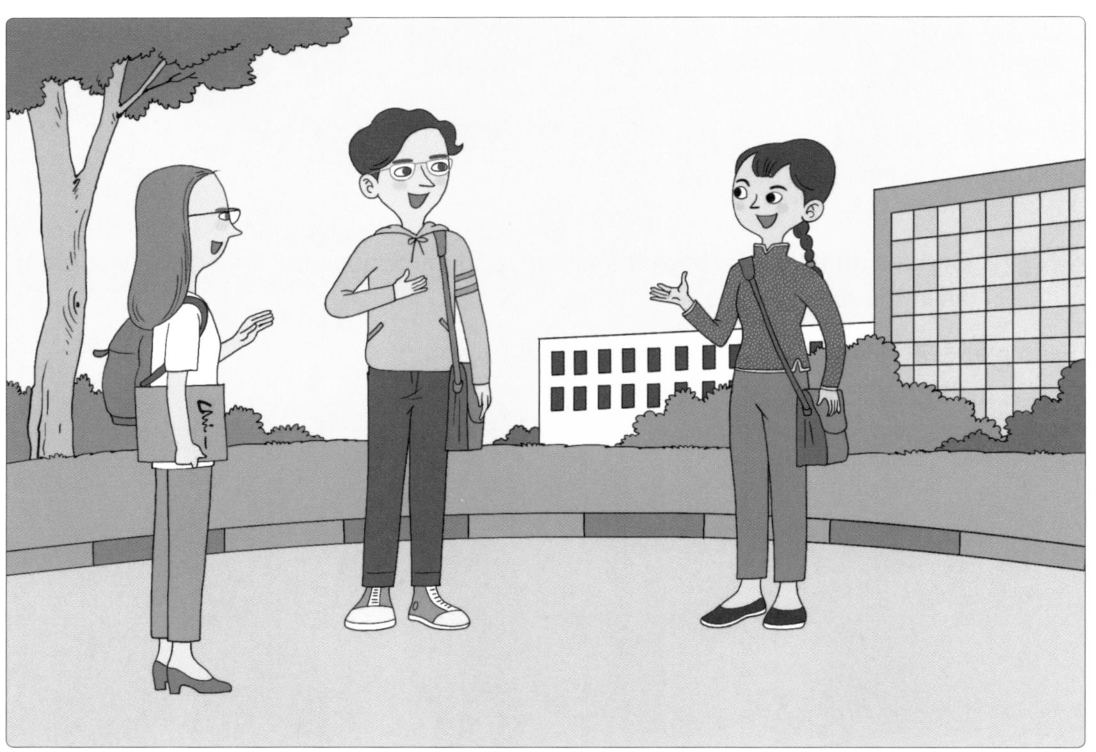

| | |
|---|---|
| 서리나 | 저는 1학년이에요. |
| 벤 | 그래요? 저도 1학년이에요. |
| 줄리아 | 저는 2학년이에요. |

| | |
|---|---|
| Cerina | I'm a first year student. |
| Ben | Is that so? I'm also a first year student. |
| Julia | I'm a second year student. |

## 문법 (Grammar) ❷

### 2-1 Copular verb '이에요/예요'

For the sentence introducing a person or an object, the copular verb '이다' (to be) is attached to the noun. The conversational forms of '이다' are '이에요' and '예요'.

| Topic | Noun + Copular verb |
|---|---|
| (1) 나는 | 벤이에요 (I am Ben. '이에요' is attached when the noun ends in a consonant.) |
| (2) 저는 | 서리나예요 (I am Cerina. '예요' is attached when the noun ends in a vowel.) |

**연습 1** Complete the sentences, writing 이에요 or 예요.

|  |  |  |  |  |
|---|---|---|---|---|
| 저는 선생님 이에요. | 저는 학생 ______. | 저는 줄리아 ______. | 저는 준 ______. | 저는 한국 사람 ______. |

**연습 2** Explain the following people as in the example.

(Example) 저는 선생님이에요. 저는 한국 사람이에요.

|  |  |  |  |
|---|---|---|---|
| 김유나 선생님/한국 | 벤/미국/1학년 | 서리나/캐나다/1학년 | 줄리아/중국/2학년 |

**연습 3** Write information about yourself in the blanks.

안녕하세요? 저는 [ ] 이에요/예요. (Write your name)

저는 [ ] 사람이에요. (한국 사람, 중국 사람, 일본 사람, 캐나다 사람, etc.)

저는 [ ] 이에요/예요. (학생, 선생님)

저는 [ ] 이에요. (1학년, 2학년, 3학년, 4학년)

**연습 4** Introduce yourself to your classmates. Include your name, nationality, status, and school year.

**Omission of topics**

Topics may be omitted when their role is obvious in the sentence.

(3) 저는 서리나예요. (저는) 1학년이에요.

**연습 5** Introduce yourself as in the example.

(Example) 안녕하세요? 저는 서리나예요. 1학년이에요.

## 2-2 The particle '도' (also)

'도' can be used as a particle so as to add the meaning of 'too' or 'also' to the subject.

| | Subject | With the topic particle은/는 | With the particle 도 |
|---|---|---|---|
| Plain form | 나 | 나는 | 나도 |
| Humble form | 저 | 저는 | 저도 |

(1) 서리나: 저는 1학년이에요. (I am a first-year student.)
벤: 저도 1학년이에요. (I am also a first-year student.)

**연습 6** Practice the following dialogue with your partner.

A: 안녕하세요? 저는 (name) 예요/이에요. 저는 (year) 학년이에요.

B: 그래요? 저도 (year) 학년이에요./ 그래요? 저는 (year) 학년이에요.

A: 저는 (nationality) 사람이에요.

B: 그래요? 저도 (nationality) 사람이에요. / 그래요? 저는 (nationality) 사람이에요.

## 말하기 (Speaking) 3. 저는 캐나다 사람이 아니에요.

| | |
|---|---|
| **줄리아** | 서리나는 캐나다 사람이에요? |
| **서리나** | 네*, 저는 캐나다 사람이에요. |
| **줄리아** | 벤도 캐나다 사람이에요? |
| **벤** | 아니요, 저는 캐나다 사람 아니에요. 미국 사람이에요. |

| | |
|---|---|
| **Julia** | Cerina, are you Canadian? |
| **Cerina** | Yes, I am Canadian. |
| **Julia** | Ben, are you Canadian, too? |
| **Ben** | No. I am not Canadian. I'm American. |

---

* '네' and '예' are both used as an interjection of the affirmative in Korea.

## 문법 (Grammar) ❸

### 3-1 '이/가 아니에요'

The copular-verb predicated in the negative Korean sentence structure is '이/가 아니에요'. The subject particle '이' is attached before the verb '아니에요' when the noun ends in a consonant, and the subject particle '가' is attached when the noun ends in a vowel.

| | | | |
|---|---|---|---|
| **Positive** | 나는 | 서리나 | 예요. (I am Cerina.) |
| **Negative** | 나는 | 서리나**가** | 아니에요. (I am not Cerina.) |

| | | | |
|---|---|---|---|
| **Positive** | 저는 | 한국 사람 | 이에요. (I am Korean.) |
| **Negative** | 저는 | 한국 사람**이** | 아니에요. (I am not Korean.) |

**연습 1 Explain each picture with your partner as in the example.**

(Example) 저는 리아가 아니에요. 저는 서리나예요.

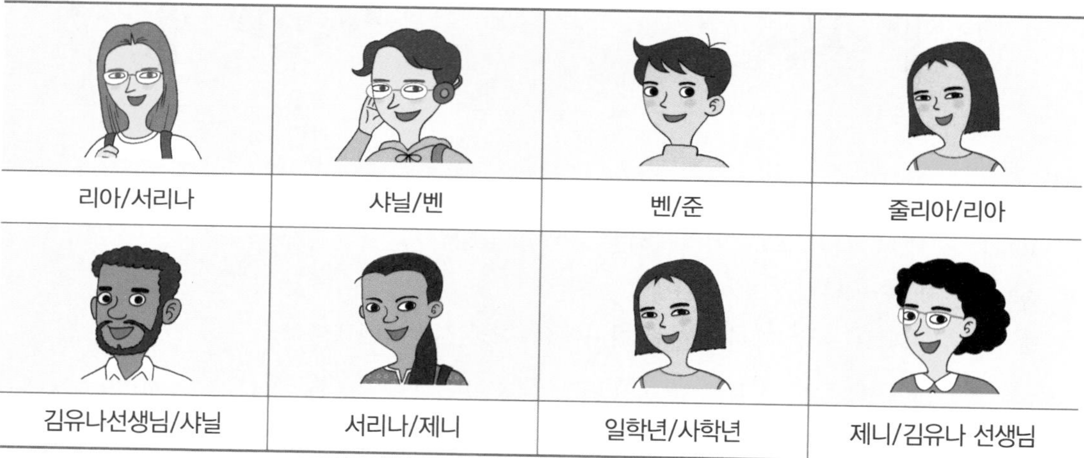

리아/서리나
샤닐/벤
벤/준
줄리아/리아
김유나선생님/샤닐
서리나/제니
일학년/사학년
제니/김유나 선생님


**연습 2 Write four negative sentences using your name, nationality, year, and status.**

(Example) 저는 서리나가 아니에요.

| | Negative sentence |
|---|---|
| Your name | |
| Your nationality | |
| Your status | |
| Your school year | |

**연습 3** **Introduce yourself to your classmates, using negative sentences as in the example.**

(Example) 안녕하세요?

| | |
|---|---|
| Name | 저는 (a different name)이/가 아니에요. |
| | 저는 (your name)예요/이에요. |
| Nationality | 저는 (a different nationality) 사람이 아니에요. |
| | 저는 (your nationality) 사람이에요. |
| Status | 저는 (a different status)이/가 아니에요. |
| | 저는 (your status)예요/이에요. |
| School year | 저는 (a different school year)학년이 아니에요. |
| | 저는 (your school year)학년이에요. |

## 3-2 '이에요/예요?'

In Korean, the word order of interrogative sentences and declarative sentences is the same. Only a '?' needs to be added to turn a declarative sentence into an interrogative. The last syllable should also be pronounced with rising intonation.
In responding, '네' or '아니요' is used in Korean. '네' means 'yes', and '아니요' means 'no'.

| | Topic + Particle | Complment + Copular-verb |
|---|---|---|
| Statement | 서리나는 | 캐나다 사람이에요. (Cerina is Canadian.) |
| Question | 서리나는 | 캐나다 사람이에요? (Is Cerina Canadian?) |

(1) 벤: 서리나는 캐나다 사람이에요? (Are you Canadian?)
서리나: 네, 저는 캐나다 사람이에요. (Yes, I am Canadian.)
(2) 서리나: 벤은 캐나다 사람이에요? (Are you Canadian?)
벤: 아니요, 저는 미국 사람이에요. (No, I am not. I am American.)

**연습 4** **Ask the following questions to three of your classmates, and fill out the table with 네 or 아니요.**

| 이름 (Name) | | | |
|---|---|---|---|
| ________ 은/는 캐나다 사람이에요? | | | |
| ________ 은/는 선생님이에요? | | | |
| ________ 은/는 1학년이에요? | | | |

**Omission of the subject particle '이/가'**

'이/가' is often omitted before '아니에요' in casual speech.

(3) 제니: 벤은 캐나다 사람이에요? (Are you Canadian?)

벤: 아니요. 저는 캐나다 사람(이) 아니에요. (저는) 미국 사람이에요.

(No, I am not Canadian. I am American.)

**연습 5** **Introduce yourself to your classmates, omitting unnecessary elements as in the example.**

안녕하세요? 저는 서리나예요.

저는 한국 사람(이) 아니에요. (저는) 캐나다 사람이에요.

저는 선생님(이) 아니에요. (저는) 학생이에요.

저는 2학년(이) 아니에요. (저는) 1학년이에요.

## 말하기 (Speaking) 4. 이름이 뭐예요?

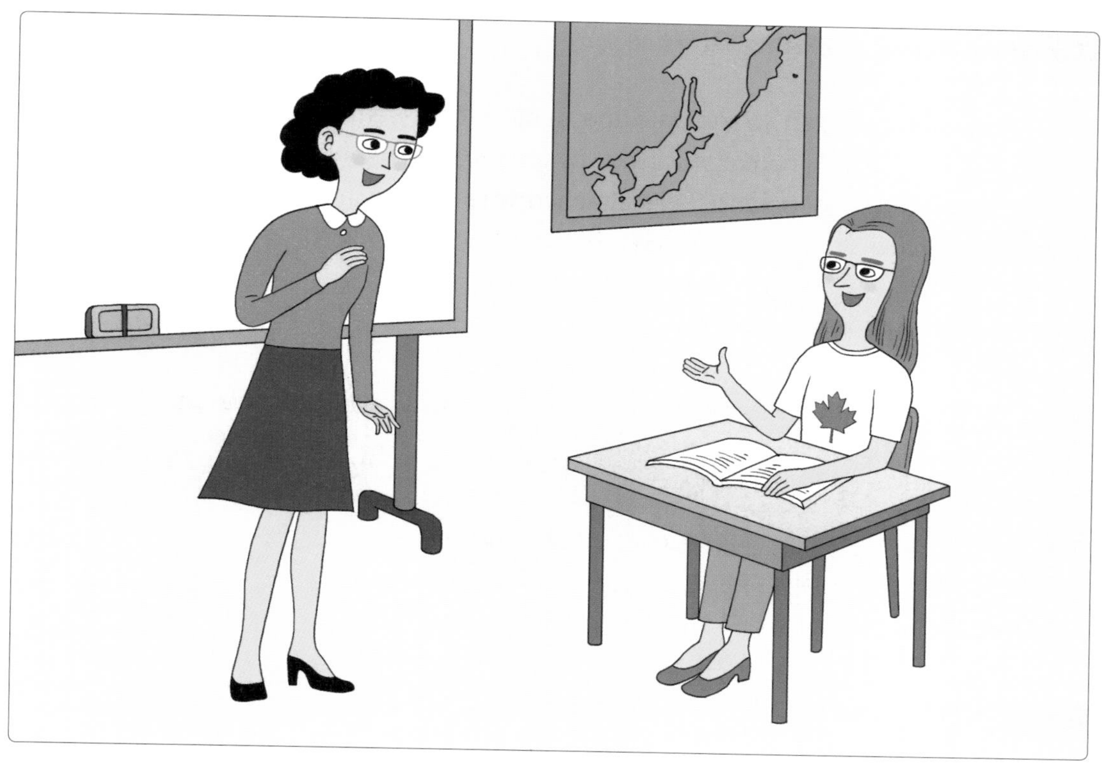

| | |
|---|---|
| **선생님** | 이름이 뭐예요? |
| **서리나** | 저는 서리나예요. |
| **선생님** | 전공이 뭐예요? |
| **서리나** | 동아시아학이에요. |

| | |
|---|---|
| **Teacher** | What's your name? |
| **Cerina** | I am Cerina. |
| **Teacher** | What's your major? |
| **Cerina** | It's East Asian Studies. |

## 문법 (Grammar) ❹

### 4-1 Subject particle '이/가'

'이/가' may also be used to indicate the subject of a sentence. Without contextual information, '이/가' has a neutral meaning. Its grammatical role is to indicate the subject of a sentence. The subject particle '이' is attached when the noun ends in a consonant, and the subject particle '가' is attached when the noun ends in a vowel.

(1) 벤이 미국 사람이에요? (Is Ben American?)
(2) 서리나가 한국 사람이에요? (Is Cerina Korean?)

When '나' (I) and '저' (I's humble form) combine with subject particles, the form changes.

• 나 + 가 (subject particle) → 내가 • 저 + 가 (subject particle) → 제가

(3) 나는 한국 사람이에요. 저는 한국 사람이에요.(I am Korean.)
(4) 나도 한국 사람이에요. 저도 한국 사람이에요. (I am also Korean.)
(5) 내가 한국 사람이에요. 제가 한국 사람이에요. (I am Korean.)

### 4-2 '은/는' vs. '이/가'

In a dialogue, '이/가' is used to indicate a certain person or object which the speaker's main interest is placed on. So when the subject is followed by the particle '이/가', the subject becomes the key or new information of the sentence.

(1) 서리나는 1학년이에요. ('1학년이에요' is the key information.)
(2) 서리나가 1학년이에요. ('서리나가' is the key information.)
(3) 선생님: 누가* 캐나다 사람이에요? (Who is Canadian? *누가: Who)
 벤: 서리나가 캐나다 사람이에요. (It is Cerina who is Canadian. '서리나' is the key information.)
(4) 선생님: 누가 캐나다 사람이 아니에요? (Who is not Canadian?)
 벤: 줄리아가 캐나다 사람이 아니에요.
 (It is Julia who is not Canadian. '줄리아' is the key information.)

**연습 1** Ask your partner the following questions.

❶ 누가* 한국 사람이에요? (*누가: Who)
❷ 누가 대학생이에요?
❸ 누가 1학년이에요?

On the other hand, '은/는' is used to introduce a general or factual statement of a certain person or a thing. So when the subject has the topic particle '은/는', the key information is not the topic, but the predicate.

(5) 서리나는 대학생이에요. (Cerina is a university student. '대학생이에요' is the key information.)
(6) 서리나는 1학년이에요. (Cerina is the first-year student. '1학년 이에요' is the key information.)
(7) 서리나는 캐나다 사람이에요. (Cerina is Canadian. '캐나다 사람이에요' is the key information.)

The topic particle '은/는' is also used when you respond with the same subject which the questioner used. As in (8) when the topic particle is used, the key information is not the subject, but the predicate, '대학생이에요'. But as in (9) when the subject particle '이/가' used, the key information is the subject, '서리나'.

(8) 벤: 서리나는 대학생이에요? (Is Cerina a university student?)
줄리아: 네, 서리나는 대학생이에요. (Yes, Cerina is a university student.)
(9) 벤: 서리나가 대학생이에요? (Is it Cerina who is a university student?)
줄리아: 네, 서리나가 대학생이에요. (Yes, it is Cerina who is a university student.)

## 4-1 '뭐예요?' (What is it?)

'뭐' is a question word which means 'What' in English. '뭐' is the colloquial form of '무엇'. In Korean language, question words stay in their original functional places, unlike English whose question words move their positions to the beginning of the sentence.

| | The subject + particle | Question word | Copular-verb |
|---|---|---|---|
| Statement | 이름이 | 서리나 | 예요 (My name is Cerina.) |
| Question | 이름이 | 뭐 | 예요? (What is your name?) |
| Question | 전공이 | 뭐 | 예요? (What is your major?) |

(1) 벤: 이름이 뭐예요? (What's your name?)
서리나: (저는) 서리나예요. (I am Cerina.)
(2) 벤: 전공이 뭐예요? (What is your major?)
서리나: 동아시아학이에요. (It is East Asian Studies.)

**Examples of majors**

| | | | |
|---|---|---|---|
| Biology<br>생물학 | Business<br>경영학 | Chemistry<br>화학 | East Asian Studies<br>동아시아학 |
| Economics<br>경제학 | Education<br>교육학 | Engineering<br>공학 | Fine Arts<br>미술 |
| Law<br>법학 | Linguistics<br>언어학 | Music<br>음악 | Nursing<br>간호학 |
| Political science<br>정치학 | Psychology<br>심리학 | Physics<br>물리학 | Science<br>과학 |

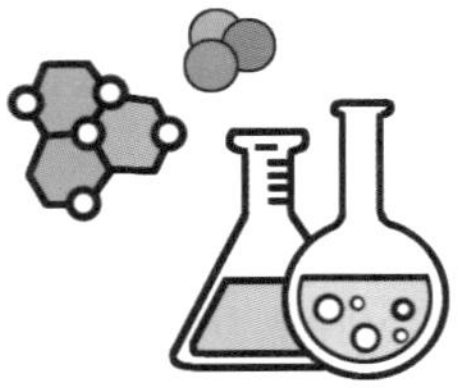

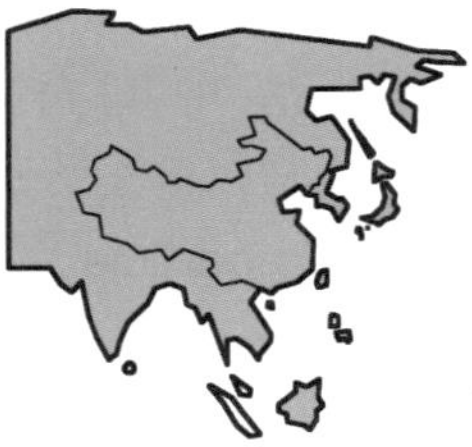

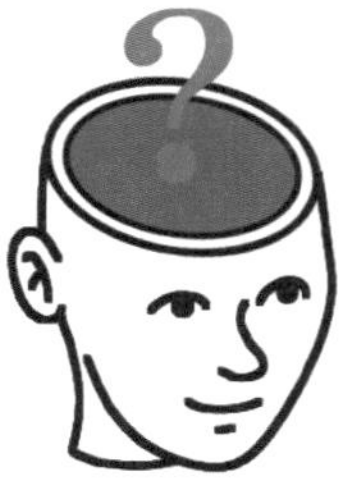

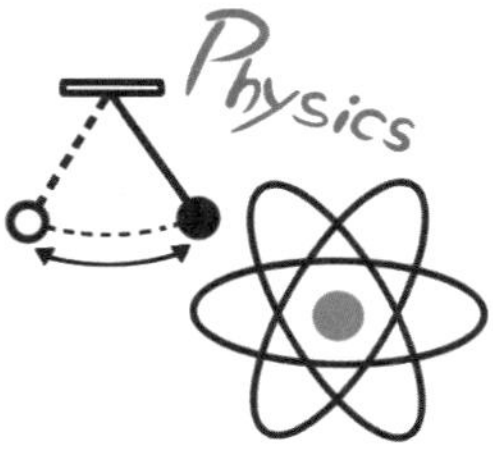

**연습 2** Interview three people. Ask their name, nationality, major, and year of studies to fill out the table.

| 이름이 뭐예요? | 일학년이에요? | 캐나다 사람이에요? | 전공이 뭐예요? |
|---|---|---|---|
| | | | |
| | | | |
| | | | |

**연습 3** Group activity ; Identification game, using the cards in the online appendix. Choose a famous person's name on your card. Your group members will ask you the suggested questions to find out who the person is. In response to their questions, explain the person's nationality, job, and gender. Finally, provide the person's name. Take turns asking and answering questions relating to the famous people until everyone has been identified.

| | | | |
|---|---|---|---|
| **Nationality** | 캐나다 사람/한국 사람/중국 사람/일본 사람/미국 사람/영국 사람 | | |
| **Job** | 가수 (singer)<br>운동 선수 (sports player)<br>대통령 (president)<br>만화 주인공 (cartoon character) | 왕자 (prince)<br>배우 (actor/actress)<br>정치가 (politician) | 사업가 [사업까] (businessman)<br>왕 (king)<br>여왕 (queen)<br>영화 감독 (movie director) |
| **Gender** | 남자/여자 | | |

1. Q: 미국 사람이에요? / 영국 사람이에요?
2. Q: 가수예요? / 운동선수예요?
3. Q: 남자예요? / 여자예요?
4. Q: 이름이 뭐예요? – This should be the last question.

## 말하기 (Speaking) 5. 이게 뭐예요?

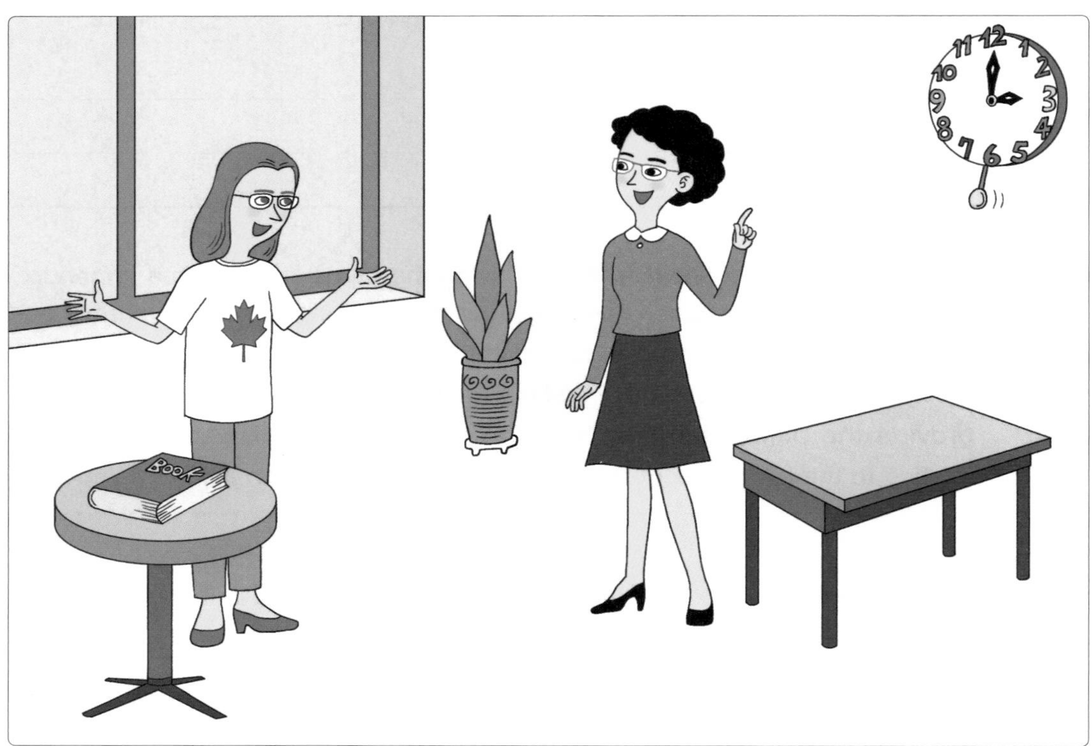


| | |
|---|---|
| **서리나** | 선생님, 이게 뭐예요? |
| **선생님** | 책이에요. |
| **서리나** | 그게 뭐예요? |
| **선생님** | 책상이에요. |
| **서리나** | 저게 뭐예요? |
| **선생님** | 시계예요. |

| | |
|---|---|
| **Cerina** | Teacher, what's this? |
| **Teacher** | It is a book. |
| **Cerina** | What's that? |
| **Teacher** | It is a desk. |
| **Cerina** | What is it over there? |
| **Teacher** | It is a clock. |

## 문법 (Grammar) ❺

### 5-1 '이/그/저'

이 (this)
Near the speaker

그 (that)
near the listener

저 (that)
away from both of the speaker and the listener

'이/그/저' (should always be used with a noun)
'이 사람', '그 사람', '저 사람' (this person, that person, that person over there)
'이 남자', '그 남자', '저 남자' (this man, that man, that man over there)

이 사과

이 가방* 그 가방*
(*가방: bag)

저 여자
저 남자

'것' means 'thing' or 'object', and can replace the noun when both the speaker and the listener are already aware of the object. '것' cannot be used to indicate a person.
'이것', '그것', '저것' (this one, that one, that one over there)
In addition, '이거', '그거', '저거' are the colloquial expressions of '이것', '그것', '저것'. When '이거', '그거', or '저거' combines with the subject particle, their forms change.

| | |
|---|---|
|  | 이게 (이것 + 이)<br>이게 뭐예요? (What's this? '이게' is the short form of '이것이') |
|  | 그게 (그것 + 이)<br>그게 뭐예요? (What's that? '그게' is the short form of '그것이') |
|  | 저게 (저것 + 이)<br>저게 뭐예요? (What is over there? '저게' is the short form of '저것이') |

**연습 1** Ask your partner about the items in your classroom, using '이게', '그게', or '저게'.

(Example) A: 이게/그게/저게 뭐예요? B: 책이에요.

| | | | | |
|---|---|---|---|---|
| 텔레비전 | 연필 | 책 | 지우개 | 모자 |
| 펜 | 의자 | 가방 | 열쇠 | 옷 |
| 시계 | 필통 | 침대 | 양말 | 전화 |
| 커피 | 돈 | 바나나 | 책상 | 꽃 |
| 사과 | 신문 | 안경 | 라디오 | 컴퓨터 |
| 칠판 | 창문 | 문 | 신발 | 물병 |

## 읽기 (Reading) 1. 안녕하세요?

서리나 안녕하세요? 저는 서리나예요.

벤 안녕하세요. 저는 벤이에요. 서리나는 캐나다 사람이에요?

서리나 네, 저는 캐나다 사람이에요. 벤도 캐나다 사람이에요?

벤 아니요, 저는 캐나다 사람 아니에요. 미국 사람이에요. 서리나는 1학년이에요?

서리나 네, 저는 1학년이에요. 벤도 1학년이에요?

벤 네, 저도 1학년이에요. 전공이 뭐예요?

서리나 동아시아학이에요.

벤 그래요? 저는 경제학이에요. 그게 뭐예요?

서리나 한국어 책이에요.

## 읽기 (Reading) 2. 저는 서리나예요.

안녕하세요? 저는 서리나예요. 저는 한국 사람이 아니에요. 캐나다 사람이에요. 저는 1학년이에요. 전공은 동아시아학이에요. 저는 한국어 반 학생이에요. 벤, 샤닐, 줄리아도 한국어 반 학생이에요. 벤은 미국 사람이에요. 샤닐은 캐나다 사람이에요. 줄리아는 중국 사람이에요. 한국어 선생님은 김유나 선생님이에요. 선생님은 한국 사람이에요. 선생님은 친절해요.

**연습 1** Respond to the following questions, using information from the reading above.

❶ 서리나는 캐나다 사람이에요?
❷ 벤은 한국어 선생님이에요?
❸ 벤도 캐나다 사람이에요?
❹ 선생님은 친절해요?

**연습 2** Write to describe yourself and your friend.

1. Introduce yourself in Korean.

2. Write about your nationality.

3. Write about your major.

4. Are you a first year student?

5. How would you describe yourself? (e.g. Are you kind? Are you friendly?)

6. Write about your friend.

## 읽기 (Reading) 1. Hello!

| | |
|---|---|
| Cerina | Hello, I am Cerina. |
| Ben | Hello, I am Ben. Are you Canadian? |
| Cerina | Yes, I am Canadian. Are you Canadian, too? |
| Ben | No, I am not Canadian. I am American. Are you a first year student? |
| Cerina | Yes, I am a first year student. Are you a first year student, too? |
| Ben | Yes, I am a first year student, too. What is your major? |
| Cerina | My major is East Asian Studies. |
| Ben | Is that so? I major in Economics. What is that? |
| Cerina | It's a Korean book. |

## 읽기 (Reading) 2. I am Cerina.

Hello, I am Cerina. I am not Korean. I am Canadian. I am a first year student. My major is East Asian Studies. I am a Korean class student. Ben, Shanil, Julia are also Korean class students. Ben is American. Shanil is Canadian. Julia is Chinese. Our Korean teacher is Yuna Kim. She is Korean. She is kind.

## 어휘 Vocabulary

### Nouns

| | |
|---|---|
| 1(일)학년 [일항년] | first year |
| 2(이)학년 [이항년] | second year |
| 3(삼)학년 [삼항년] | third year |
| 4(사)학년 [사항년] | fourth year |
| 경제학 | economics |
| 남자 | man |
| 대학생 [대학쌩] | university student |
| 동아시아학 | East Asian studies |
| 미국 | America |
| 반 | class |
| 사람 | person |
| 선생님 | teacher |
| 시계 | watch, clock |
| 여자 | woman |
| 영국 | England |
| 영어 | English |
| 음악 [으막] | music |
| 이름 | name |
| 일본 | Japan |
| 전공 | major |
| 중국 | China |
| 책 | book |
| 책상 [책쌍] | desk |
| 캐나다 | Canada |
| 학생 [학쌩] | student |
| 한국 | Korea |
| 한국어 [한구거] | Korean language |

### Verbs

| | |
|---|---|
| 아니다 (아니에요) | not to be |
| 이다 (이에요/예요) | to be |

### Adjectives

| | |
|---|---|
| 반갑다 (반가워요) | to be glad |
| 안녕하다 (안녕하세요) | hello |
| 친절하다 | to be kind |

### Other expressions

| | |
|---|---|
| 그래요 | to be so |
| 네 | yes |
| 무엇/뭐 | what |
| 아니요 | no |
| 이거/그거/저거 | this/that/that thing over there |
| 과 | lesson |
| 저 (humble) / 나 (plain) | I |

Memo

Lesson

# 3

# 어디에 있어요?

(Where is it?)

Lesson

# 3 어디에 있어요? (Where is it?)

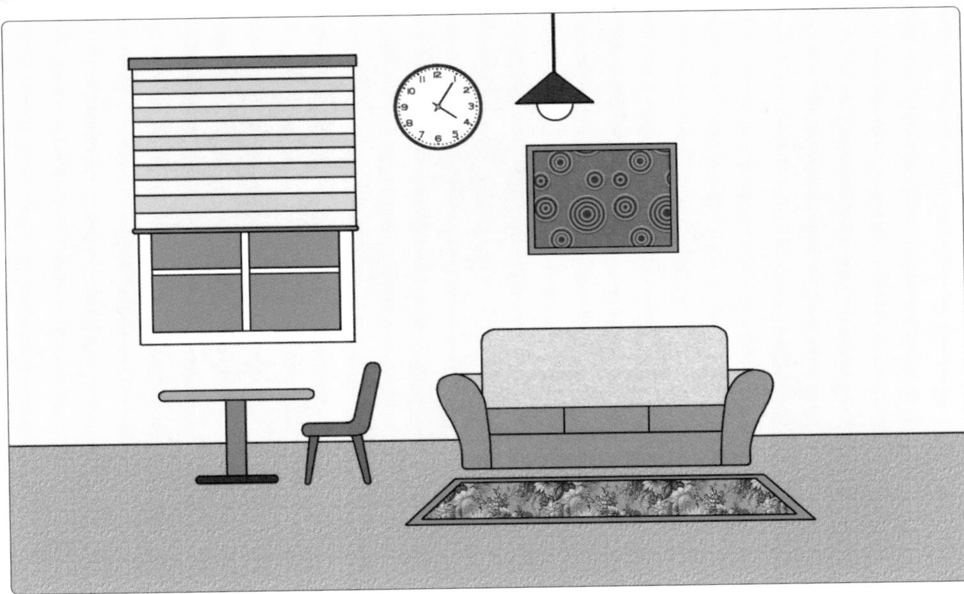

말하기 1 학교 식당이 어디에 있어요? (Where is the school cafeteria?)

말하기 2 섭 빌딩하고 토리 빌딩 안에는 뭐가 있어요?
(What is in the SUB building and the Tory building?)

말하기 3 지금 뭐 해요? (What are you doing now?)

말하기 4 대학교가 어때요? (How's the university?)

Upon completion of this lesson, you will be able to:

1. Describe the locations of items
2. Describe daily activities
3. Describe the qualities of objects

**Grammatical items**

- 어디 있어요? (Where is it?)
- 앞, 옆, 위, 밑, 뒤, 안, 밖 (Relative position)
- 에 (Locative particle)
- 은/는 (Topic particle)
- –어요/아요/여요 (Polite ending)
- 하고 (Particle for joining nouns)
- 그리고, 그런데 (Conjunction for connecting sentences)

## 표현 (Expressions)

| | |
|---|---|
| 고맙습니다<br> | Thank you.<br><br>벤: 이거 선물*이에요. (This is a gift for you. *선물: gift)<br>서리나: 고맙습니다 (Formal) / 고마워요 (Informal) / 고마워 (Intimate) |
| 감사합니다<br> | Thank you.<br><br>(After a speech)<br>감사합니다 (Formal) / 감사해요 (Informal polite) |
| 미안합니다<br> | I am sorry.<br><br>벤: 미안합니다 (Formal) / 미안해요 (Informal) / 미안해 (Intimate)<br>서리나: 괜찮습니다 (Formal) / 괜찮아요 (Informal) / 괜찮아 (Intimate)<br>(It's okay.) |
| 죄송합니다<br> | I am sorry. (A formal apology which is usually used when talking to seniors)<br><br>(Ben was late for the class.)<br>벤: 선생님, 죄송합니다 (Formal) / 죄송해요 (Informal polite) |

**연습** **Practice the dialogues below with your classmates.**

(1) Giving a present to your classmate

A: 이거 선물*이에요. (*선물: gift)

B: 고맙습니다 / 고마워요 / 감사합니다 / 감사해요.

(2) After bumping into a person

A: 미안합니다 / 미안해요 / 죄송합니다 / 죄송해요.

B: 괜찮습니다 / 괜찮아요.

## 문화 (Culture)

### Responses to expressions of gratitude and apologies

In English, there are specific responses to expressions of gratitude or apologies, such as 'You're welcome,' 'That's okay,' 'No problem,' etc. Korean has similar types of responses, as shown in the table below.

| | 감사합니다 / 고맙습니다 | 죄송합니다 / 미안합니다 |
|---|---|---|
| **Response** | 별 말씀을…<br>뭘요<br>천만에요 | 괜찮습니다 |

However, if you said '고맙습니다' to express your gratitude in Korea, many Koreans would respond with a smile, instead of a particular response. This is because many Koreans feel that those responses are too stiff or too formal to express their sincerity. Facial expression is often considered more important than the expression of those formal saying in Korea.

## 발음 (Pronunciation) 'ㅎ' weakening

The consonant 'ㅎ' tends to become silent between two voiced sounds such as vowels, nasals, or [ㄹ] in colloquial speech.

삼학년 (Nasalization) → [삼항년] ('ㅎ' weakening) → [삼앙년] (Resyllabification) → [사망년]
일학년 (Nasalization) → [일항년] ('ㅎ' weakening) → [일앙년] (Resyllabification) → [이랑년]

**연습 1** **Write the pronunciation of the following according to their sound.**

(Example) 전화 [저놔]

| | | | |
|---|---|---|---|
| 일학년 | | 이학년 | |
| 삼학년 | | 사학년 | |
| 많아요 | | 사랑한다 | |
| 괜찮아요 | | 좋아요 | |
| 잘했어요 | | 안녕하세요 | |

## 말하기 (Speaking) 1. 학교 식당이 어디에 있어요?

서리나 학교 식당이 어디 있어요?
제니 도서관 옆에 있어요.
서리나 한국어 교실은 어디 있어요?
제니 토리 빌딩 안에 있어요.

Cerina Where is the school cafeteria?
Jenny It's beside the library.
Cerina Where is the Korean classroom?
Jenny It's in the Tory building.

## 문법 (Grammar) ❶

### 1-1 '어디 있어요?' (Where is it?)

In asking for the location of an item, the question word '어디' is used. In referring to the location of an item, the locative particle '에' is used with the existential verb '있다 (있어요)'.

(1) 벤: 서리나가 어디에 있어요? (Where is Cerina?)
    줄리아: (서리나는) 우체국에 있어요. (She is at the post office.)

The locative particle may be omitted when it is used with '어디' in a sentence.

(2) 한국어 책이 어디(에) 있어요? (Where is the Korean book? – Written form)

(3) 서리나: 벤, 한국어 책이 어디 있어요? (Ben, where is the Korean book? – Casual speech form)
    벤: (한국어 책은) 가방 안에 있어요. (It's in the bag.)

**연습 1** **Explain where Cerina is, using the following places.**

A: 서리나가 어디 있어요?

B: 은행*에 있어요. (*은행: bank, 병원: hospital)

**연습 2** **Make dialogues about the following places as in the example.**

A: 에드먼턴이 어디 있어요?

B: 캐나다에 있어요.

❶ 에드먼턴 (Edmonton) ❷ 토론토 (Toronto) ❸ 서울 (Seoul) ❹ 런던 (London)
❺ 베이징 (Beijing) ❻ 파리 (Paris) ❼ 로마 (Rome) ❽ 모스코바 (Moscow)

## 1-2 Relative position

A location may be further specified with words of relative position, indicating front, back, side, inside, outside, under, or above.

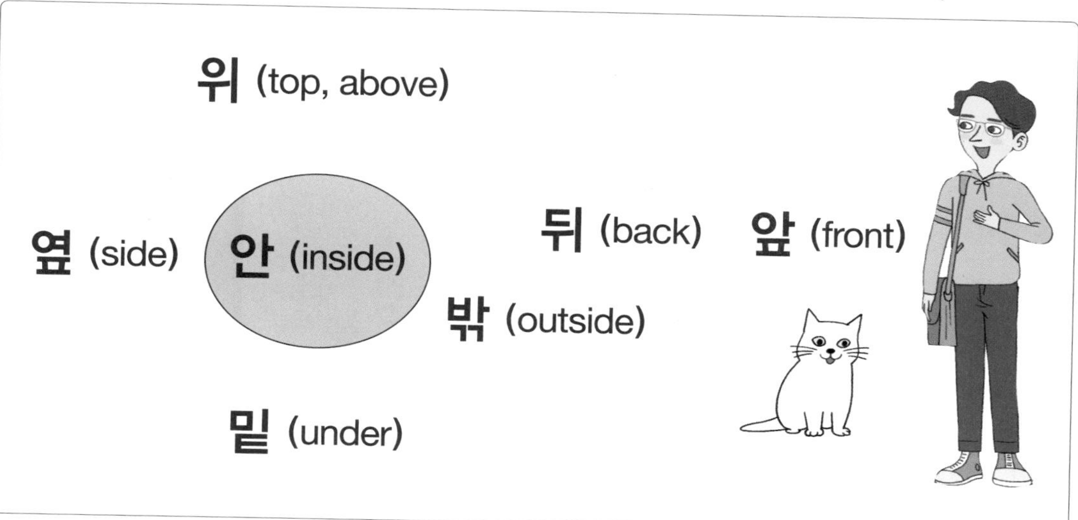


(1) 서리나: 고양이가 어디 있어요? (Where is the cat?)
　줄리아: 벤 옆에 있어요. (It is beside Ben.)

| Subject | Centre Location | Relative position | Locative particle | Verb of existence |
|---|---|---|---|---|
| 고양이가 | 서리나 | 뒤 | 에 | 있어요 (The cat is behind Cerina.) |
| 책이 | 가방 | 안 | 에 | 있어요 (The book is in the bag.) |
| 우체국이 | 도서관 | 옆 | 에 | 있어요 (The post office is beside the library.) |

**연습 3** Explain the location of a cat while moving it around you and your classmate. (Material in the online appendix)

A: 고양이가 어디 있어요?

B: [　　　　] 에 있어요.

**연습 4** Ask and respond. Take turns asking about the location of each item with your partner.

가방, 모자, 시계, 연필, 우산, 의자, 지우개, 창문 (window), 책, 책상, 칠판, 문 (door), 고양이, 컴퓨터 (computer), 선생님, 휴지통 (trash can)

**연습 5** Ask and respond. Take turns asking about the location of each building with your partner as in the example.

(Example) A: 아츠 빌딩이 어디 있어요?

B: 토리 빌딩 옆에 있어요.

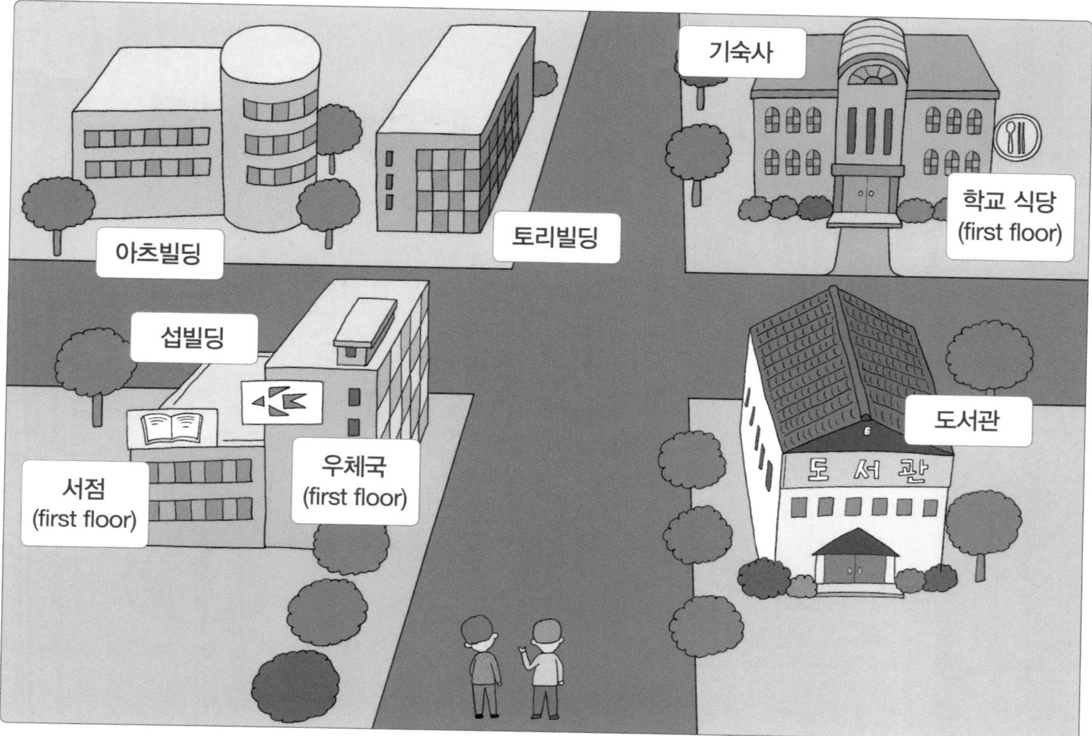


**연습 6** You and your classmate have a picture of the same room, but with different items inside the room. Find the location of each item in your partner's picture by asking questions. The picture is in the online appendix.

## 말하기 (Speaking) 2. 섭 빌딩에 뭐가 있어요?

| | |
|---|---|
| **서리나** | 섭 빌딩에 뭐가 있어요? |
| **벤** | 서점하고 우체국이 있어요. |
| **서리나** | 그럼, 헙 빌딩에는 뭐가 있어요? |
| **벤** | 식당하고 기숙사가 있어요. |

| | |
|---|---|
| Cerina | What is in the SUB building? |
| Ben | There is a bookstore and a post office. |
| Cerina | Then, what is in the HUB building? |
| Ben | There is a restaurant and a dormitory. |

## 문법 (Grammar) ❷

### 2-1 (Place) '에 뭐가 있어요?'

(1) 뭐가 있어요? (What is there?)
(2) 서리나: 방에 뭐가 있어요? (What is in the room?)
벤: (방에) 책상이 있어요. (There is a desk in the room.)
(3) 서리나: 책상 위에 뭐가 있어요? (What is on the desk?)
벤: 가방이 있어요. (There is a bag.)

**연습 1** Ask the following questions and respond using the items in the picture.

❶ 교실에 뭐가 있어요?
❷ (Partner's Name) 방에 뭐가 있어요?
❸ 도서관에 뭐가 있어요?

| | | | | |
|---|---|---|---|---|
| 텔레비전 | 연필 | 책 | 지우개 | 모자 |
| 펜 | 의자 | 가방 | 열쇠 | 옷 |
| 시계 | 필통 | 침대 | 양말 | 전화 |
| 커피 | 돈 | 바나나 | 책상 | 꽃 |
| 사과 | 신문 | 안경 | 라디오 | 컴퓨터 |
| 칠판 | 창문 | 문 | 신발 | 물병 |

**연습 2** Ask about the locations of items in the picture, using '뭐,' as in the example.

(Example) A: 선생님, 책상 위에 뭐가 있어요? B: 컴퓨터가 있어요.

**연습 3** Role play: Julia and Cerina are living in a same neighbourhood. First, start with asking the name of the building which is located beside the other person's house, as in the example. And then find the locations of all the buildings as well as the locations of Julia and Cerina. The materials are in the online appendix.

줄리아: 서리나 집 옆에 뭐가 있어요?
서리나: 집 옆에 은행이 있어요.

## 2-2 Topic particle: '은/는'

'은/는' should be added to the subject when the topic has changed.

(1) 서리나: 학교 식당이 어디 있어요? (Where is the school cafeteria?)
벤: (학교 식당은) 도서관 옆에 있어요. (It is beside the library.)
서리나: 그럼, 도서관은 어디 있어요? (Then, where is the library?)
벤: (도서관은) 아츠 빌딩 옆에 있어요. (It's beside the Arts Building.)

(2) 서리나: 섭 빌딩에 뭐가 있어요? (What is in the SUB building?)
벤: 서점이 있어요. (There is a bookstore.)
서리나: 그럼, 헙 빌딩에는* 뭐가 있어요? (What is in the HUB building?)

벤: 식당이 있어요. (There is a restaurant.)

* A location may be the topic, and a topic particle '은/는' is added to the locative particle '에'.

(3) 서리나: 이게* 뭐예요? (What is this? *'이게' is the short form of '이것이')

벤: 시계예요. (It's a watch.)

서리나: 그럼, 그건* 뭐예요? (What is that? *'그건' is the short form of '그것은')

벤: 가방이에요. (It's a bag.)

- 그것 + 은 → 그건 (short form for casual speech)
- 이것 + 은 → 이건
- 저것 + 은 → 저건

**연습 4** Ask and respond. Take turns asking and answering questions about personal belongings or items in the classroom.

A: 이게/그게/저게 뭐예요?

B: [ ] 예요/이에요.

A: 그럼, 이건/그건/저건 뭐예요?

B: [ ] 예요/이에요.

'은/는' is also used to contrast one topic with another.

| 캐나다 사람 | 캐나다 사람 | 한국 사람 |
|---|---|---|

(4) 서리나는 캐나다 사람이에요. 샤닐도 캐나다 사람이에요. 그런데* 준은 한국 사람이에요. (*그런데: but)
(Cerina is Canadian. Shanil is also Canadian. But Jun is Korean.)

**연습 5** Interview your classmates. Ask at least 5 classmates about their school years and nationalities, and find one classmate whose school year is different from the others. Explain what you found to your partner.

| Name | | | | | |
|---|---|---|---|---|---|
| Year | | | | | |
| Nationality | | | | | |

❶ (Name)은/는 [ ] 학년이에요. (Name)도 [ ] 학년이에요.

그런데* (Name)은/는 [ ] 학년이에요. (*그런데: but)

❷ (Name)은/는 [ ] 사람이에요. (Name)도 [ ] 사람이에요.

그런데 (Name)은/는 [ ] 이에요.

## 2-3 The particle '하고' for joining nouns

'하고' is used when connecting more than two nouns in casual speech.

(1) 벤: 방 안에 뭐가 있어요? (What is in the room?)
서리나: 책상하고 의자가 있어요. (There is a desk and a chair.)

(2) 벤: 이 빌딩 안에 뭐가 있어요? (What is in this building?)
서리나: 서점하고 우체국이 있어요. (There is a bookstore and a post office.)

**연습 6** Ask your partner the following questions. Respond using '하고'.

❶ (Name) 가방 안에 뭐가 있어요?
❷ (Name) 방에 뭐가 있어요?
❸ 교실 안에 뭐가 있어요?
❹ 이 빌딩 안에 뭐가 있어요?

| | | | | |
|---|---|---|---|---|
| 텔레비전 | 연필 | 책 | 지우개 | 모자 |
| 펜 | 의자 | 가방 | 열쇠 | 옷 |
| 시계 | 필통 | 침대 | 양말 | 전화 |
| 커피 | 돈 | 바나나 | 책상 | 꽃 |
| 사과 | 신문 | 안경 | 라디오 | 컴퓨터 |
| 칠판 | 창문 | 문 | 신발 | 물병 |

## 3. 지금 뭐 해요?

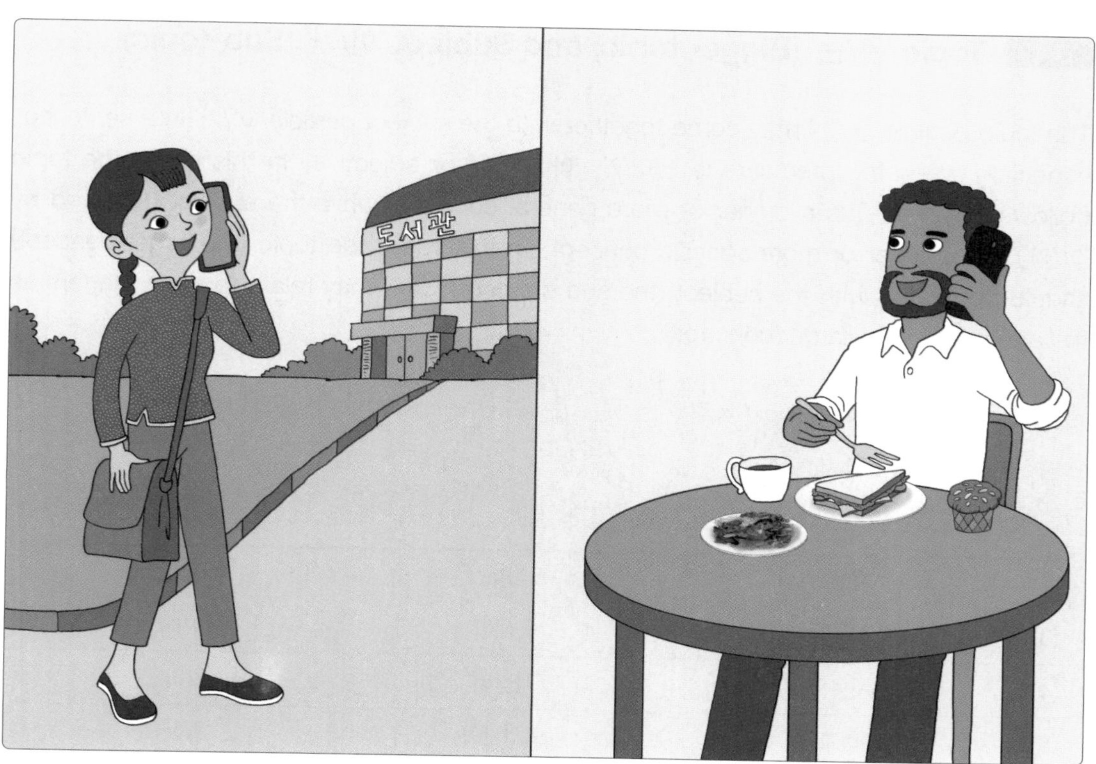


**줄리아** 샤닐, 지금 뭐 해요?

**샤닐** 아침 먹어요. 학교 식당은 음식이 아주 맛있어요. 줄리아는 지금 뭐 해요?

**줄리아** 저는 도서관에 가요.

**Julia** Shanil, what are you doing now?

**Shanil** I am eating breakfast. The school cafeteria has delicious food. What are you doing?

**Julia** I am going to the library.

## 문법 (Grammar) ❸

### 3-1 Topic '은/는' (Bigger topic) and Subject '이/가' (Sub-topic)

The topic particle '은/는' may come together with the subject particle '이/가' in a sentence, especially when the predicate is '있어요', '아니에요', or adjective. In this case, the topic (followed by '은/는') is a bigger or more general concept, while the subject (followed by '이/가') is a smaller or more specific concept. In this case, the topic (the larger concept) should be related with the subject (the sub concept), and may relate to such matters as the attributes of the larger concept.

(1) Seoul has many people.
서울은 사람이 많아요.

(2) University has large libraries.
대학교는 도서관이 커요.

| | Topic | subject | predicate |
|---|---|---|---|
| (3) | 학교 식당은 | 음식이 | 싸요. |
| (4) | 서울은 | 사람이 | 많아요. |
| (5) | 대학교는 | 도서관이 | 좋아요. |

**연습 1** Complete the translation of the following sentences into Korean.

- The university has many libraries. → 대학교는 ______.
- The school cafeteria has delicious coffee. → 학교 식당은 ______.
- I have many friends. → 저는 ______.
- The library has big desks. → 도서관은 ______.

**연습 2** Make 5 sentences by combining the topic cards, the subject cards, and the predicate cards. (See the materials in the online appendix)

| Topic + 은/는 | Subject + 이/가 | predicate |
|---|---|---|
| 학교 식당은 | 음식이 | 싸요 |
| **Topic** | **Subject** | **predicate** |
| | | |

| Topic | Subject | predicate |
|---|---|---|
| | | |

| Topic | Subject | predicate |
|---|---|---|
| | | |

| Topic | Subject | predicate |
|---|---|---|
| | | |

| Topic | Subject | predicate |
|---|---|---|
| | | |

## 3-2 Verbs and adjectives

Verbs generally describe actions and processes, while adjectives describe states, such as size, weight, quality, etc. While English adjectives should come with a copular verb to be a predicate, Korean adjectives conjugate independently as verbs do.

- Examples of verbs: 먹다, 앉다, 가다
- Examples of adjectives: 괜찮다, 좋다, 크다

Verbs and adjectives are composed of a stem and an ending '다'. In conjugation, the stem is not changed, but the ending is changed according to the speech style. '다' is attached to verb and adjective stems only in the basic form.

| Copular verbs | | Verbs | | Adjectives | |
|---|---|---|---|---|---|
| Stem | Ending | Stem | Ending | Stem | Ending |
| 이 | 다 | 하 | 다 | 넓 | 다 |
| 아니 | 다 | 인사하 | 다 | 있 | 다 |
| | | 먹 | 다 | 맛있 | 다 |
| | | 숙제하 | 다 | 많 | 다 |
| | | 자 | 다 | 괜찮 | 다 |
| | | 앉 | 다 | 좋 | 다 |

## 3-3 The polite ending '-어요/아요/해요'

The polite ending '어요/아요/해요' is most commonly used in conversation.

❶ '아요' is attached to the stem when the last vowel of the stem has a bright vowel ('아',or '오').

| Dictionary form | | | Polite form | |
|---|---|---|---|---|
| stem | ending | | stem | ending |
| 좋 | 다 | → | 좋 | 아요 |
| 많 | 다 | → | 많 | 아요 |

앉다 [ ] 괜찮다 [ ]

❷ '어요' is attached to the stem when the last vowel of the stem has a dark vowel (NOT '아', or '오').

| Dictionary form | | | Polite form | |
|---|---|---|---|---|
| stem | ending | | stem | ending |
| 먹 | 다 | → | 먹 | 어요 |
| 있 | 다 | → | 있 | 어요 |

맛있다 [ ] 넓다 [ ]

❸ '여요' is attached when the verbs or adjectives include '하다'. In this case, '하여요' is contracted into '해요'. 하다 → 하여요 → 해요

| Dictionary form | | | Polite form | |
|---|---|---|---|---|
| stem | ending | | stem | ending |
| 인사하 | 다 | → | 인사해요 | |
| 공부하 | 다 | → | 공부해요 | |

숙제하다 [ ] 전화하다(to call) [ ]

❹ Copular verbs have their own polite forms.

| Dictionary form | | | Polite form | |
|---|---|---|---|---|
| stem | ending | | stem | ending |
| 이 | 다 | → | 학생 (The noun ending in a consonant) | 이에요 |
| | | | 모자 (The noun ending in a vowel) | 예요 |
| 아니 | 다 | → | 아니에요 | |

이다 [ ] 아니다 [ ]

## 3-4 '뭐 해요?' (What are you doing?)

Question word, '뭐' can be used together with the verb '해요?'

(1) 서리나가 뭐 해요? (What is Cerina doing?)

(2) 벤: 서리나, 지금 뭐 해요? (Cerina, what are you doing now?)
서리나: 숙제해요. (I'm doing homework.)

**연습 3** Look at the pictures and practice the following dialogue with your partner.

| | | | |
|---|---|---|---|
| 공부해요 (to study) | 아침 먹어요 | 학교에 가요 | 숙제해요 |
| 책 읽어요 (to read a book) | 이야기해요 | 자요 | |
| 전화해요 (to make a call) | 주스* 먹어요 (*주스: juice) | 의자에 앉아요 | |

A: 서리나가 뭐 해요?

B: 자요.

**연습 4** Ask your partner about what s/he is going to do today.

A: (Name), 오늘 뭐 해요?

B: ______________.

| 이름 | | | | |
|---|---|---|---|---|
| | | | | |

**연습 5** Interview your classmate with the following questions.

A: (Name), 매일 한국어 공부해요?

B: 네. / 아니요.

1. 매일* 한국어 공부하다 (*매일 공부하다: to study everyday) 네 ( ), 아니요 ( )
2. 매일 책 읽다 네 ( ), 아니요 ( )
3. 매일 전화하다* (*전화하다: make a call) 네 ( ), 아니요 ( )
4. 매일 학교에 가다* (*가요 is the polite form of 가다) 네 ( ), 아니요 ( )
5. 늦게* 자다 (*늦게: late, 자요 is the polite form of 자다) 네 ( ), 아니요 ( )
6. 햄버거*가 좋다 (*햄버거: hamburger) 네 ( ), 아니요 ( )
7. 핸드폰*이 있다 (*핸드폰: cellphone) 네 ( ), 아니요 ( )
8. 방이 넓다 네 ( ), 아니요 ( )
9. 숙제가 많다 네 ( ), 아니요 ( )
10. 커피가 맛있다 네 ( ), 아니요 ( )
11. 학교 식당 음식이 싸다* (*싸요 is the polite form of 싸다) 네 ( ), 아니요 ( )

## 말하기 (Speaking) 4. 대학교가 어때요?

| | |
|---|---|
| **리아** | 대학교가 어때요? |
| **서리나** | 재미있어요. 그리고 학생도 많아요. |
| **리아** | 그래요? 수업은 어때요? |
| **서리나** | 아주 좋아요. 그런데 숙제가 조금 많아요. |

| | |
|---|---|
| **Lea** | How is the university? |
| **Cerina** | It's fun. And it has many students. |
| **Leah** | Really? How are your classes? |
| **Cerina** | Very good. But I have a lot of homework (than I expected). |

## 문법 (Grammar) ❹

### 4-1 '어때요?' (How is it?)

'어때요?' is used to ask the other person's opinion about an object. It means 'how is (it)? The dictionary form of '어때요' is '어떻다'.

(1) 학교 식당이 어때요? (How is the school cafeteria?)

(2) 도서관이 어때요? (How is the library?)

The adverbs '아주 (very)', and '조금 (a little)' may be used in front of the adjectives to express the degree of the state. But when '조금' comes with the adjective '많다,' it does not mean 'a little'. '조금 많다' means 'more than the speaker expected'.

(3) 리아: 한국어가 어때요? (How is Korean language?)
    서리나: 아주 재미있어요. (It is very interesting.)

(4) 리아: 숙제가 많아요? (Do you have a lot of homework?)
    서리나: 네, 조금 많아요. (Yes, I have quite a lot of homework (more than I expected)).

**연습 1** **Ask the following questions to your classmate, and answer them using the suggested words and '아주/조금'.**

❶ 학교 식당 음식이 어때요?
❷ 도서관이 어때요?
❸ 한국어가 어때요?
❹ 커피가 어때요?
❺ (Name) 친구가 어때요?
❻ 한국어 교실이 어때요?
❼ 한국어 선생님이 어때요?
❽ 학교 기숙사가 어때요?

- 좋아요/나빠요
- 넓어요/좁아요 (to be narrow)
- 맛있어요/맛없어요 (to be not tasty)
- 싸요/비싸요 (to be expensive)
- 재미있어요/재미없어요 (to be not interesting)
- 커요/작아요
- 바빠요 (to be busy)
- 예뻐요 (to be pretty)

### 4-2 The conjunction '그리고'

The conjunction '그리고' connects two sentences and has the meaning of 'and'.

(1) 대학교 도서관은 커요. 대학교 도서관은 넓어요.
    → 대학교 도서관은 커요. 그리고 (대학교 도서관은) 넓어요.
    (The university library is big. And it is spacious.)

(2) 서리나는 친절해요. 서리나는 똑똑해요.* (*똑똑하다: to be smart)
    → 서리나는 친절해요. 그리고 똑똑해요. (Cerina is kind. And she is smart.)

(3) 서리나: 학교 식당이 어디 있어요? (Where is the school cafeteria?)
벤: 섭 빌딩 안에 있어요. 그리고 헙몰 안에도 있어요.
(It's in the SUB building. And it is also in the HUB building.)

(4) 서울은 커요. 그리고 (서울은) 사람이 많아요. (Seoul is big. And it has many people.)

(5) 학교 식당은 커피가 싸요. 그리고 (학교 식당은 커피가) 맛있어요.
(The coffee of the school cafeteria is cheap. And it is tasty.)

**연습 2** **Choose two adjectives and describe each person in the picture using '그리고', as in the example. Then, describe your personality using '그리고'.**

(Example) 서리나는 예뻐요. 그리고 귀여워요.

| | | |
|---|---|---|
| 예뻐요 (to be pretty) | 잘 생겼어요 (to be handsome) | 귀여워요 (to be cute) |
| 착해요 [차캐요] (to be nice) | 친절해요 (to be kind) | 부지런해요 (to be diligent) |
| 용감해요 (to be brave) | 명랑해요 (to be cheerful) | 똑똑해요 [똑또캐요] (to be smart) |
| 사교적이에요 (to be social) | 적극적이에요 (to be active) | 조용해요 (to be quiet) |

## 4-3 The conjunction '그런데'

The conjunction '그런데' connects the two sentences with two different meanings according to the context; (1) 'but', (2) 'by the way'.

(1) 리아: 한국어는 재미있어요?
서리나: 네, 재미있어요. 그런데 경제학은 재미없어요.
(Yes, it is interesting. But Economics is not interesting.)
리아: 오늘 한국어 숙제가 있어요?
서리나: 아니요, 없어요. 그런데 경제학은 숙제가 많아요.

(2) 서리나: 저는 오늘 학교에 가요. 그리고 친구를 만나요.
벤: 그래요? 그런데 친구는 한국 사람이에요? (그런데: by the way)
(Really? By the way, is your friend Korean?)
서리나: 네, 한국 사람이에요.

**연습 3** Each sentence has two related sentences which can be connected with (1) '그리고' and (2) '그런데'. Find the two related sentences, using the sentences in the online appendix.

❶ 한국어 반이 재미있어요.

(1) 그리고 ______________________.

(2) 그런데 ______________________.

❷ 오늘 경제학 수업이 있어요.

(1) 그리고 ______________________.

(2) 그런데 ______________________.

❸ 제 남자친구는 친절해요.

(1) 그리고 ______________________.

(2) 그런데 ______________________.

❹ 벤은 서리나를 좋아해요.

(1) 그리고 ______________________.

(2) 그런데 ______________________.

❺ 저는 오늘 학교에 가요.

(1) 그리고 ______________________.

(2) 그런데 ______________________.

## 읽기 (Reading) 1. 뭐 해요?

**리아** 안녕, 서리나. 지금 뭐 해요?
**서리나** 한국어 숙제해요.
**리아** 한국어가 재미있어요?
**서리나** 네, 아주 재미있어요. 그런데 숙제가 조금 많아요. 리아는 어디 가요?
**리아** 섭 빌딩에 가요.
**서리나** 그래요? 섭빌딩은 어디 있어요?
**리아** 도서관 옆에 있어요. 섭빌딩에 학교 식당하고 우체국하고 서점이 있어요.
**서리나** 학교 식당 음식은 어때요?
**리아** 맛있어요. 그리고 커피도 싸요.

## 읽기 (Reading) 2. 서리나 집은 대학교 기숙사예요.

서리나 집은 대학교 기숙사예요. 기숙사 방이 넓어요. 서리나 방에는 책상하고 의자가 있어요. 책상 위에는 한국어 책하고 연필이 있어요. 책상 밑에는 가방이 있어요.
서리나는 지금 한국어 숙제해요. 한국어가 아주 재미있어요. 그런데 숙제가 조금 많아요.
리아는 서리나 룸메이트*예요. 리아는 지금 학교 식당에 가요. 학교 식당은 섭빌딩 안에 있어요.
학교 식당 음식이 싸요. 그리고 맛있어요.

* 룸메이트: roommate

**연습 1** The following questions are about 읽기 2. Respond to the questions.

1. 서리나 집이 어디예요?
2. 학교 식당이 어디 있어요?
3. 학교 식당 음식이 어때요?
4. 서리나가 지금 뭐해요?

**연습 2** Write to describe your room and classroom.

1. How is your room? (e.g. Is it big? Is it clean?)

2. What is in your room? Where are those items located in your room?

3. Where is the Korean classroom located?

4. What items are there in the Korean classroom?

## 읽기 (Reading) 1. What are you doing?

**Leah** Hi Cerina, what are you doing?

**Cerina** I'm doing the Korean homework.

**Leah** Is Korean interesting?

**Cerina** Yes, it is very interesting. But it has lots of homework. Where are you going?

**Leah** I'm going to the SUB building.

**Cerina** Really? Where is the SUB building?

**Leah** It is beside the library. In the SUB building, there is a school cafeteria, post office, and a bookstore.

**Cerina** How is the food of the school cafeteria?

**Leah** It is delicious. And the coffee is cheap.

## 읽기 (Reading) 2. Cerina's place is a university dormitory.

Cerina's place is a university dormitory. The dormitory room is big. There is a desk and a chair in Cerina's room. There is a Korean book and a pencil on the desk. There is a bag under the desk. Cerina is doing her Korean homework now. Korean is very interesting. But it has quite a bit of homework. Leah is Cerina's roommate. Leah is going to the school cafeteria now. The school cafeteria is in the SUB building. The school cafeteria food is cheap. And it is delicious.

## 어휘 Vocabulary

### Nouns

| | |
|---|---|
| 가방 | bag |
| 고양이 | cat |
| 기숙사 [기숙싸] | dormitory |
| 교실 | classroom |
| 대학교 [대학꾜] | college, university |
| 도서관 | library |
| 모자 | hat |
| 방 | room |
| 빌딩 | building |
| 서점 | bookstore |
| 수업 | class |
| 식당 [식땅] | restaurant |
| 아침 | breakfast, morning |
| 연필 | pencil |
| 우산 | umbrella |
| 우체국 | post office |
| 음식 | food |
| 의자 | chair |
| 지우개 | eraser |
| 집 | house, home |
| 칠판 | blackboard |
| 커피 | coffee |
| 학교 [학꾜] | school |

### Verbs

| | |
|---|---|
| 가다 | to go |
| 먹다 | to eat |
| 숙제(하다) [숙쩨하다] | to do homework |
| 앉다 [안따] | to sit |
| 이야기 (하다) | to talk |
| 자다 | to sleep |
| 하다 | to do |

### Adjectives

| | |
|---|---|
| 괜찮다 [괜찬타] | to be all right |
| 나쁘다 | to be bad |
| 넓다 [널따] | to be spacious |
| 많다 [만타] | to be many |
| 맛있다 [마싣따] | to be delicious |
| 싸다 | to be cheap |
| 있다 | to be (existence) |
| 작다 | to be small (size) |
| 재미있다 | to be interesting |
| 좋다 [조타] | to be good |
| 크다 | to be big |

### Other expressions

| | |
|---|---|
| 그럼 | then |
| 아주 | very |
| 지금 | now |
| 조금 | a little |
| 어때요 | how (is it)? |
| 어디 | where |
| 에 | at (locative particle) |
| 뒤 | the back |
| 밑 | the bottom |
| 밖 | the outside |
| 안 | the inside |
| 앞 | the front |
| 옆 | the side |
| 위 | the upper |

Memo

Lesson

# 4

# 시간 있으세요?

(Do you have time?)

# 시간 있으세요? (Do you have time?)

말하기 1 오늘 시간이 있어요? (Do you have time today?)

말하기 2 누구세요? (Who is it?)

말하기 3 앉으세요. (Please sit.)

말하기 4 누가 서리나 뒤에 있어요? (Who is behind Cerina?)

말하기 5 뭘 먹어요? (What do you eat?)

Upon completion of this lesson, you will be able to:

1. Explain the possession of items
2. Use honorific forms to seniors or people at a higher position
3. Make a command or request
4. Make a sentence using transitive verbs

**Grammatical items**

- –이/가 있다/없다 (Possessive verbs)
- 그래서 (Conjunction – therefore)
- –(으)세요 (Honorific ending)
- –지 마세요 (Negative imperative ending)
- 누구 / 누가 (Question words)
- –을/를 (Object particle)

## 표현 (Expression) 요즘 어떻게 지내세요?

**서리나** 안녕하세요? 선생님.

**선생님** 안녕하세요? 서리나. 요즘 어떻게 지내요?

**서리나** 잘 지내요. 선생님은 요즘 어떻게 지내세요?

**선생님** 저는 조금 바빠요. 서리나는 지금 어디 가요?

**서리나** 저는 우체국에 가요.

**선생님** 그래요? 그럼, 안녕히 가세요.

**서리나** 네, 안녕히 계세요.

| | |
|---|---|
| **요즘 어떻게 지내세요?** | How are you doing these days? The general response are (1) '잘 지내요' (I'm doing good). (2) '좀 바빠요' (I'm somewhat busy). (3) '그저 그래요' (Just so so). |
| **안녕히 가세요.** | Lit. Go in peace. Good bye. (using it to the person who is leaving) |
| **안녕히 계세요.** | Lit. Stay in peace. Good bye. (using it to the person who is staying) |

**연습**

Practice the above dialogue with your partner, changing the underlined parts according to your situation.

## 문화 (Culture)

In Korea, addressing a person by his or her name is not culturally allowed when the person is older or in a higher position. This cultural formality tends to be strictly practiced even when the age difference between the speaker and the listener is very small. The following address terms are generally used when the speaker needs to call a person whose age or status is higher.

| 선생님 | 사모님 | 여사님 | 어르신 | 사장님 |
|---|---|---|---|---|
| A person whose age or position is higher than the speaker | The wife of a man whose age or position is higher than the speaker | A woman whose age or position is higher than the speaker; it is close to 'Mrs.' in English. | Honorific form of elder people. | A person whose age or position is higher than the speaker; it is usually used to address a person who is running a business. |

'저기요', '여기요', '저기', '이보세요', 이봐요 are also used to call a stranger. In fact, '당신' is the honorific pronoun of '너'(you), however, the use of '당신' (you) is culturally prohibited except in love relationships, because '당신' also the contradictory usage of lowering a person in argument.

| | | | |
|---|---|---|---|
|  | 당신, 사랑해.<br>(Honey, I love you.) |  | 당신, 뭐야! (You! What are you?) |

## 발음 (Pronunciations)

'맛있다', and '맛없다' were originally composed of two words (맛 + 있다/없다). Thus, the words should be pronounced as [맏 + 읻따] → [마딛따] and [맏 + 업따] → [마덥따]. However, the pronunciation of '맛있다' has changed into [마싣따] over the years. The National Institute of Korean Language accepts both [마싣따] and [마딛따] as Korean standard language. On the other hand, '맛없다' keeps its original pronunciation [마덥따].

맛있어요 ______　　　　맛없어요 ______

## 말하기 (Speaking) 1. 오늘 시간이 있어요?

| | |
|---|---|
| **서리나** | 준, 오늘 시간 있어요? |
| **준** | 아니요, 없어요. 오늘은 수업이 많아요. 그래서 바빠요. |
| **서리나** | 그럼, 내일은 어때요? |
| **준** | 내일은 괜찮아요. |

| | |
|---|---|
| **Cerina** | Jun, do you have any free time today? |
| **Jun** | No, I don't. I have a lot of classes. So I'm busy. |
| **Cerina** | Then, how about tomorrow? |
| **Jun** | Tomorrow is okay with me. |

## 문법 (Grammar) ❶

### 1-1 '이/가 있어요/없어요'

'있다' is also used to mean the possession of an item. The possessed item acts as the subject in the sentence. Non-possession is expressed by '없다'.

(1) I have an apple.
저는 사과가 있어요.

(2) I don't have a class.
저는 수업이 없어요.

**연습 1** Complete the translation of the following sentences into Korean.

- I have a book. → 저는 ________.
- I have a banana. → 저는 ________.
- I have homework. → 저는 ________.
- Cerina has a bag. → 서리나는 ________.
- Ben has a class. → 벤은 ________.

(3) 서리나: 벤, 오늘 수업이 있어요? (Ben, do you have a class today?)
벤: 아니요, 오늘 수업이 없어요. (No, I don't have a class today.)

(4) 선생님: 질문이 있어요? (Do you have a question?)
서리나: 네, 있어요. 오늘 숙제가 있어요? (Yes, I do. Do we have any homework today?)
선생님: 아니요, 없어요. (No, you don't.)

**Omission of the subject particle '이/가'**

The subject particle '이/가' may be omitted before '있어요/없어요' in casual speech.

(5) 벤은 여자 친구(가) 없어요. (Ben doesn't have a girlfriend.)

(6) 서리나: 벤, 여자 친구 있어요? (Ben, do you have a girlfriend?)
벤: 아니요, 없어요. (No, I don't have.)

**연습 2** Look at the pictures and ask your classmates if they have these items.

A: (Name), 의자 있어요?
B: 네, 있어요. / 아니요, 없어요.

케이크
가방
시계
볼펜
우산
빵
바나나
모자
SNU
돈
사과
지갑
지우개
ERASE


## 1-2 '있어요/없어요' vs. '이에요/아니에요'

In Korean, '이에요/예요/아니에요' (copular verbs) can be used only for the meaning of equation and identification, as shown in the examples of (1) and (2) below. This is different from English which may use copular verbs to describe the existence or the possession of objects which are shown in the examples provided in (3) and (4).

**'이에요/예요/아니에요'**

(1) Identification: 저는 서리나예요. (I am Cerina.)

- 저는 서리나 있어요. (Unnatural)

이건 사전이에요. (This is a dictionary.)

(2) Equation: 벤은 학생이에요. (Ben is a student.)

- 벤은 학생 있어요. (Unnatural)

벤은 선생님이 아니에요. (Ben isn't a teacher.)

**'있어요/ 없어요'**

(3) Existence: 서리나는 학교에 있어요/없어요. (Cerina is at school. / Cerina isn't at school.)

- 서리나는 학교에 이에요. (Unnatural)

– Copular verbs cannot be used for the meaning of existence.

(4) Possession: 서리나는 교과서가 있어요/없어요.
(Cerina has a textbook. / Cerina doesn't have a textbook.)

- 서리나는 교과서예요. (Unnatural)

– Copular verbs cannot be used for the meaning of possession.

**연습 3** Find the wrong part and change it to make a correct sentence.

❶ 서리나는 학생 있어요. → [          ].

❷ 서리나는 1학년 있어요. → [          ].

❸ 서리나는 도서관이에요. → [          ].

❹ 벤은 도서관에 이에요. → [          ].

❺ 학교 식당은 섭빌딩에 이에요. → [          ].

❻ 저는 마이클 옆에 이에요. → [          ].

## 1-3 The conjunction '그래서'

The conjunction '그래서' connects two sentences with the meaning of 'so', or 'therefore'. '그래서' indicates a cause-effect relation between two sentences.

(1) 저는 오늘 수업이 없어요. 그래서 친구를 만나요.
(I don't have a class today. So I meet a friend.)

(2) 저는 내일도 수업이 없어요. 그래서 내일은 집에 있어요.
(I don't have a class tomorrow, either. So I will be at home tomorrow.)

**연습 4** Tony does not have a class today and tomorrow. He calls Ben, but he is not at home. Tony feels lonely. Read Tony's narrative and fill in the blanks with appropriate conjunctions ('그리고', '그래서', or '그런데').

저는 오늘 수업이 없어요. [          ] 집에 있어요.
저는 내일도 수업이 없어요. [          ] 텔레비전을 봐요.
[          ] 텔레비전이 재미없어요. [          ] 전화해요.
[          ] 친구 벤이 집에 없어요. 벤은 요즘 아주 바빠요.
요즘 저는 돈도 없어요. [          ] 재미없어요.
저는 여자 친구도 없어요. [          ] 쓸쓸해요*. 냉장고*에 음식도 없어요.
[          ] 저는 배고파요!*

(*쓸쓸해요: lonely, 냉장고: refrigerator, 배고파요: hungry)

## 말하기 (Speaking) 2. 누구세요?

| | |
|---|---|
| **서리나** | 똑똑! (knocking on the door of 선생님's office) |
| **선생님** | 누구세요? |
| **서리나** | 저는 서리나예요. |
| **선생님** | (Opens the door) 안녕하세요? 서리나. |
| **서리나** | 선생님, 지금 시간 있으세요? |
| **선생님** | 네, 괜찮아요. |

| | |
|---|---|
| **Cerina** | Knock! Knock! |
| **Teacher** | Who is it? |
| **Cerina** | I'm Cerina. |
| **Teacher** | Hi, Cerina. |
| **Cerina** | Teacher, do you have time now? |
| **Teacher** | Sure. It's fine. |

## 문법 (Grammar) ❷

### 2-1 The honorific ending: '–(으)세요'

The honorific ending '–(으)세요' is used for three different purposes to show your respect; (1) when talking to seniors, such as your teacher, or your grandparents, (2) when talking about seniors, and (3) when asking a request.

(1) 선생님, 연구실에 가세요? (Are you going to the office?) → Talking to seniors
(2) 선생님은 연구실에 가세요. (My teacher is going to the office.) → Talking about seniors
(3) 벤, 연구실에 가세요. (Ben, go to the office.) → Asking a request

'–(으)시다' is the dictionary form. It includes the honorific marker '시'. '–(으)시다' is added right after the stem of the predicate. '–(으)시다' is the dictionary form of the honorific ending, and '–(으)세요' is the speech form of honorific ending.

| –으세요 (after a consonant) | | –세요 (after a vowel) | |
|---|---|---|---|
| 재미있 | 으세요 | 가 | 세요 |
| 앉 | 으세요 | 인사하 | 세요 |
| 읽 | 으세요 | 크 | 세요 |

**연습 1 A and B are politely talking to each other, using the honorific ending. Practice the following dialogue with your partner using the honorific ending whenever it is needed.**

A: (Name), 오늘 시간이 있어요?
B: 아니요, 없어요. 오늘 수업이 있어요. (Name)도 오늘 수업이 있어요?
A: 아니요, 없어요. (Name)은/는 오늘 숙제가 많아요?
B: 네, 아주 많아요.
A: 수업은 재미있어요?
B: 네, 아주 재미있어요. (Name)은/는 내일 바빠요?
A: 아니요. 내일은 수업이 없어요. 그래서 한국 식당에 가요.
B: 그래요? (Name)은/는 한국 음식 좋아해요?
A: 네, 아주 좋아해요. (Name)도 내일 한국 식당에 가요?
B: 아니요. 저는 내일 친구 집에 가요.

**연습 2 Ask your partner the following questions, using the honorific ending.**

❶ (Name)은/는 한국 사람이에요?
❷ (Name)은/는 2학년이에요?

3. (Name)은/는 한국어가 재미있어요?
4. (Name)은/는 오늘 수업이 많아요?
5. (Name)은/는 오늘 어디에 가요?
6. (Name)은/는 오늘 뭐 해요?
7. (Name)은/는 요즘 뭐 읽어요?
8. (Name)은/는 강아지*가 있어요? (*강아지: dog)
9. (Name)은/는 고양이 좋아해요?
10. (Name), 시간 있어요?

## 2-2 '누구' (Who)

'누구' is a question word which means 'who'.

(1) 누구예요? (Who is it?)

(2) 누구세요? (Honorific form)

(3) 서리나: 저는 오늘 리아를 만나요. (I meet Leah today.)
벤: 리아가 누구예요? (Who is Leah?)
서리나: 리아는 룸메이트예요. (Leah is my roommate.)

(4) 벤: (똑똑) (Knocking)
서리나: 누구세요? (Who is it?)
벤: 저예요. 벤이에요. (It's me, Ben.)

**연습 3** **You and your friend are knocking on the door of a Korean teacher's office. Role play a student and a teacher, using the following dialogue.**

Student: 똑똑!
Teacher: 누구세요?
Student: 저는 (Name)이에요/예요.
Teacher: 그래요? (Opens the door and find out that there is someone else with the student.)
Teacher: 누구예요? (Pointing to the other person)
Student: (Friend's name)이에요/예요. (Name of a course) 수업 학생이에요.
Teacher: 그래요? 들어 오세요*. (*들어 오다: to come in)

**연습 4** **Practice the following dialogue with your partner.**

A: (Name), 내일 수업 있어요?
B: 네, (Name of a course) 수업이 있어요.
A: (Name of the course) 수업은 재미있어요?
B: 네, 아주 재미있어요. 선생님도 좋으세요.
A: 선생님이 누구세요?
B: (Name of the instructor) 선생님이세요.

## 말하기 (Speaking) 3. 앉으세요.

| | |
|---|---|
| **선생님** | 앉으세요. 그리고 책 펴세요. |
| | (Ben is talking with a classmate.) |
| **선생님** | 벤, 수업 시간에 이야기하지 마세요. |
| **벤** | 죄송합니다. |

| | |
|---|---|
| **Teacher** | Please sit. And open the book. |
| **Teacher** | Please don't talk with a friend during class time. |
| **Ben** | I am sorry. |

## 문법 (Grammar) ❸

### 3-1 Making a request, using '-(으)세요'

The honorific ending is also used for making a request respectfully.

(1) 서세요. (Please stand up)

(2) 앉으세요. (Please sit down.)

(3) 여기 보세요. (Please look here.)

(4) 인사하세요. (Please greet each other.)

(5) 책 펴세요. (Please open the book).

(6) 책 읽으세요. (Please read the book.)

(7) 따라하세요. (Please repeat after me.)

(8) 열심히 공부하세요. (Please study hard.)

**연습 1** Make requests to your classmates, using the above sentences.

### 3-2 '-지 마세요' (Negative command)

'-지 마세요' is the negative imperative sentence ending, and can be translated as 'don't…'. The dictionary form of '마세요' is '말다' which means 'to stop' or 'to cease'. '-지 마세요' is used to prohibit or dissuade someone from taking an action.

(1) 학교에 가세요 (Go to school). → 학교에 가지 마세요 (Don't go to school).

**연습 2** Practice making negative commands with your partner, using the pictures.

(*보다: to see, 운전하다: to drive, 노래하다: to sing, 식사하다: to have a meal, 주다: to give, 춤을 추다: to dance)

**연습 3** The teacher is angry because of the students. Please ask the students to behave well in the classroom, using '-지 마세요'.

(Example) 줄리, 수업에 늦지 마세요.

수업에 늦다 (to be late at class)
사진을 찍다 (to take a picture)
자다
담배를 피우다 (to smoke)
전화하다
책상 위에 앉다
껌을 씹다 (to chew the gum)
노래하다 (to sing)
모자를 쓰다 (to wear a hat)
음식을 먹다
이야기하다

## 말하기 (Speaking) 4. 누가 서리나 뒤에 있어요?

선생님 누가 서리나 뒤에 있어요?
제니 샤닐이 서리나 뒤에 있어요. 저는 서리나 옆에 있어요.
선생님 잘 했어요*. 그럼, 누가 1학년이에요?
줄리아 제가 1학년이에요.

Teacher Who is behind Cerina?
Jenny Shanil is behind Cerina. I am beside Cerina.
Teacher Good job! Then, who is a first year student?
Julia I am a first year student.

---

*잘 했어요: Good job!

## 문법 (Grammar) ❹

### 4-1 '누가' (Who + the subject particle '가')

When '누구' is attached to the subject particle '가', '누가' is used instead of '누구가'.
'누구' (as subject) + '가' (the subject particle) → '누가'

(1) 선생님: 누가 교실에 있어요? (Who is in the classroom?)
    벤: 서리나가 교실에 있어요. (Cerina is in the classroom.)
(2) 누가 서리나 뒤에 있어요? (Who is behind Cerina?)
(3) 누가 K-POP 좋아해요? (Who likes K-POP?)
(4) 누가 집에 고양이가 있어요? (Who has a cat at home?)
(5) 누가 키*가 커요? (Who is tall?) (*키: height)

Note: Some adjectives are not compatible with '누가', such as '넓다', '맛있다', '싸다'.

**연습 1** Ask your partner the following questions.

❶ 누가 교실에 있어요?
❷ 누가 ____________ 뒤/옆/앞에 있어요?
❸ 누가 K-POP 좋아해요?
❹ 누가 집에 고양이가 있어요?

**연습 2** Make dialogues about each picture, using the expressions in the box.

A: 누가 공부해요? B: 토니가 공부해요.

| 공부하다 | (밥) 먹다 | 물 마시다 (마셔요) | 학교에 가다 | 숙제하다 | |
|---|---|---|---|---|---|
| 인사하다 | 책 읽다 | 자다 | 전화하다 | 친구를 만나다 | |
| 한국 사람이다 | 캐나다 사람이다 | 집에 있다 | 교실에 있다 | 수영하다 | 바쁘다 |

| | | | | |
|---|---|---|---|---|
| 벤 | 서리나 | 제니 | 벤 | 샤닐 |
| 리아 | 줄리아 | 토니 | 준 | 마크 |

## 말하기 (Speaking) 5. 뭘 먹어요?

준 벤, 아침에 뭘 먹어요?
벤 저는 빵 먹어요. 준은 뭘 먹어요?
준 저는 밥 먹어요. 저는 밥이 맛있어요.
벤 저는 아침에 커피 마셔요. 준은 뭘 마셔요?
준 저는 차 마셔요.

Jun Ben, what do you eat for breakfast?
Ben I eat bread. What do you eat, Jun?
Jun I eat rice. I find rice more delicious.
Ben I drink coffee in the morning. What do you drink, Jun?
Jun I drink tea.

## 문법 (Grammar) ⑤

### 5-1 The object particle '-을/를'

**What is an object?**
Objects are the elements of a sentence which transitive verbs describe. A transitive verb is a verb that requires one or more objects.

Some verbs always need objects in a sentence.
(1) I eat breakfast. 먹다 (저는 밥을 먹어요.)
(2) I watch TV. 보다* (저는 TV를 봐요.) *보다: to watch; *봐요: polite form of '보다'
(3) I drink juice. 마시다 (저는 주스를 마셔요.)
(4) I know Cerina. 알다 (저는 서리나를 알아요.)

Some predicates do not need objects in a sentence.
(5) I go to school. ('to school' is an adverb phrase.) 가다 (저는 학교에 가요.)
(6) I sleep at home. ('at home' is an adverb phrase.) 자다 (서리나는 집에서* 자요.)
*집에서: at home
(7) I sit on the chair. ('on the chair' is an adverb phrase.) 앉다 (저는 의자에 앉아요)

All adjectives, copular verbs, and possessive verbs do not need objects.
(8) 저는 학생이에요. (I am a student. Copular verb)
(9) 저는 학생이 아니에요. (I am not a student. Copular verb)
(10) 저는 바빠요. (I am busy. Adjective)
(11) 옷이 커요. (The clothes are big. Adjective)
(12) 저는 학교에 있어요. (I am at school. Existence)
(13) 저는 컴퓨터가 있어요. (I have a computer. Possession)

**연습 1** Check all the predicates which need an object.

| | | | | |
|---|---|---|---|---|
| 가다 | 공부하다 | 마시다 | 만나다 | 먹다 |
| 보다 | 아니다 | 앉다 | 없다 | 예쁘다 |
| 이다 | 있다 | 자다 | 크다 | |

'-을/를' is attached to the noun acting as the object in the sentence. '-을' is attached when the stem of the verb ends with a consonant, while '-를' is attached when the stem of the verb ends with a vowel.

(14) 서리나가 아침을 먹어요. (Cerina eats breakfast.)
(15) 벤이 텔레비전을 봐요. (Ben watches TV.)
(16) 서리나가 커피를 마셔요. (Cerina drinks coffee.)
(17) 벤이 친구를 만나요. (Ben meets a friend.)
(18) 저는 사과를 좋아해요. (I like apples.)
(19) 저는 사과가 좋아요. (The literal meaning: For me, apple is good.)

The sentences (18) and (19) have similar meaning in Korean. However, '좋아하다' is a transitive verb which means 'to like', and must be followed by an object. On the other hand, '좋아요' is an adjective which means 'nice'/'good', and comes with a subject.

- 저는 사과를 좋아요. (unnatural)
- 저는 사과가 좋아해요. (unnatural)

**연습 2** **Look at the pictures, and ask your partner questions using the words from the box, as in the example.**

A: 벤은 지금 뭐 해요?
B: 친구를 만나요.

Objects: 교과서, 밥, 숙제, 물, 책, 친구, 텔레비전, 한국어, 수영, 노래 (song)
Verbs: 공부해요, 마셔요, 만나요, 먹어요, 읽어요, 해요, 봐요 (to watch)

**연습 3** **Ask your partner the following questions.**

1. 뭘(뭐를) 좋아해요? (1) 사과 (2) 바나나 (3) 케이크 (4) 아이스크림 (5) 피자
2. 뭐가 좋아요? (1) 텔레비전 (2) 컴퓨터 (3) 핸드폰 (cell phone) (4) 차 (car)
3. 누굴(누구를) 좋아해요? (1) 피터팬 (2) 스파이더맨 (3) 배트맨 (4) 슈퍼맨 (5) 아이언맨
4. 누가 좋아요? (1) 신데렐라 (2) 뮬란 (3) 포카혼타스 (4) 해리포터 (5) 엘사

The omission of the object particle sounds more natural in casual speech, so it is common to omit the particles in conversation.

(20) 서리나는 오늘 친구를 만나요. (Cerina is meeting a friend today.)

(21) 벤: 서리나, 오늘 뭐 하세요? (Cerina, what are you doing today?)
서리나: 친구 만나요. (I am meeting a friend.)

(22) 벤: 내일 뭐 공부하세요? (What do you study tomorrow?)
서리나: 한국어 공부해요. (I study Korean.)

**연습 4** **Interview your classmates with the following questions. Respond in casual talk, omitting unnecessary particles.**

| 이름이 뭐예요? | 오늘 뭐 해요? | 오늘 뭐 먹어요? | 오늘 뭐 마셔요? | 오늘 누구 만나요? | 오늘 뭐 공부해요? |
|---|---|---|---|---|---|
| | | | | | |
| | | | | | |
| | | | | | |

## 읽기 (Reading) 1. 한국 영화를 좋아해요

| | |
|---|---|
| **벤** | 안녕? 준, 요즘 어떻게 지내요? |
| **준** | 좀 바빠요. 요즘 시험이 많아요. 벤은 지금 어디 가요? |
| **벤** | 토리 빌딩에 가요. 한국 문화 수업이 있어요. |
| **준** | 한국 문화 수업은 어때요? |
| **벤** | 재미있어요. 요즘 한국 영화를 공부해요. |
| **준** | 그래요? 선생님이 누구세요? |
| **벤** | 권우찬 선생님이세요. 선생님이 아주 좋으세요. |
| **준** | 그래요? 저도 한국 영화 좋아해요. 벤, 내일 시간 있어요? |
| **벤** | 네, 왜요? |
| **준** | 내일 커피 마셔요. 그리고 한국 영화 이야기도 해요. |
| **벤** | 네, 좋아요. 그럼 내일 만나요. 시험 공부 잘 하세요. |

## 읽기 (Reading) 2. 한국 문화 수업

벤은 오늘 한국 문화 수업이 있어요. 권우찬 선생님이 한국 문화 수업을 가르치세요. 교실에는 학생이 많아요. 한국 문화 수업 시간에 벤은 한국 영화하고 문화를 공부해요. 한국 영화하고 문화 이야기는 아주 재미있어요. 벤은 한국 문화 수업을 아주 좋아해요. 그래서 벤은 열심히 공부해요. 지금 벤은 도서관에 가요. 도서관에 준이 있어요. 준은 한국어 수업 조교*예요. 준도 한국 영화를 좋아해요. 그래서 벤하고 준은 한국 영화 이야기를 많이 해요. 그런데 준은 오늘 시간이 없어요. 그래서 벤하고 준은 내일 만나요.

---

*조교: teaching assistant

**연습 1** Read the narration and respond to the following questions.

1. 준은 뭘* 좋아해요? (*뭘: the short form of '뭐를')
2. 누가 한국 문화 수업을 가르치세요?
3. 한국 문화 수업 시간에 뭘 공부해요?
4. 벤은 왜 열심히 공부해요?
5. 벤하고 준은 지금 어디 있어요?

**연습 2** Write to describe your favorite items and activities.

1. What do you like? (e.g. movies, sports, pets, or personal belongings)

2. Write about your favorite actor or sports player. Why do you like them?

3. What do you usually do on weekends?

4. What is your favorite food?

5. What classes do you have this term? How are those classes?

## 읽기 (Reading) 1. I like Korean movies.

**Ben** Hi Jun, How are you doing these days?

**Jun** Quite busy. I have many exams these days. Where are you going now?

**Ben** I'm going to the Tory building. I have the Korean culture class.

**Jun** How is the Korean culture class?

**Ben** It is interesting. We are studying Korean movies these days.

**Jun** Is that so? Who is the teacher?

**Ben** It is Mr. Wu-Chan Kwon. He is very nice.

**Jun** Is that so? I like Korean movies, too. Do you have time tomorrow?

**Ben** Yes, I do. Why?

**Jun** Let's have coffee tomorrow. And let's talk about Korean movies, too.

**Ben** Sure. Then, see you tomorrow. Work hard with your exam.

## 읽기 (Reading) 2. Korean culture class

Ben has the Korean culture class today. Mr. Wu-Chan Kwon teaches the Korean culture class. The class has lots of students. Ben studies Korean movies and culture in the Korean culture class. The stories of Korean movies and culture are very interesting. Ben likes the Korean culture class very much, so he studies hard. Now Ben is going to the library. He will meet Jun in the library. Jun is a teaching assistant for a Korean language class. Jun also like Korean movies. So Ben and Jun often talk about Korean movies. But Jun does not have time today. So Ben and Jun will meet tomorrow.

## 어휘 Vocabulary

### Nouns

| | |
|---|---|
| 교과서 | textbook |
| 내일 | tomorrow |
| 돈 | money |
| 문화 | culture |
| 물 | water |
| 밥 | meal |
| 볼펜 | ball-point pen |
| 빵 | bread |
| 사과 | apple |
| 사전 | dictionary |
| 시간 | time |
| 시험 | test, exam |
| 연구실 | professor's office |
| 영화 | movie |
| 오늘 | today |
| 옷 | clothes |
| 주스 | juice |
| 지갑 | wallet |
| 질문 | question |
| 차 | tea |
| 친구 | friend |
| 컴퓨터 | computer |
| 텔레비전 | television |

### Verbs

| | |
|---|---|
| 가르치다 | to teach |
| 공부(하다) | to study |
| 들어오다 | to come in |
| 마시다 | to drink |
| 만나다 | to meet |
| 말다 (말아요) | to stop |
| 수영(하다) | to swim |
| 알다 | to know |
| 인사(하다) | to greet |
| 읽다 [익따] | to read |
| 전화(하다) | to call |
| 좋아하다 | to like |
| 지내다 | to get along |

### Adjectives

| | |
|---|---|
| 맛없다 [마덥따] | to be not tasty |
| 바쁘다 | to be busy |
| 없다 | (1) to not be (existence) |
| | (2) to not have |
| 있다 | to have |
| 재미없다 | to be uninteresting |

### Other expressions

| | |
|---|---|
| 누구 | who |
| 누굴 (누구를) | who |
| 똑똑 | knock, knock! |
| 많이 [마니] | a lot |
| 뭘 (뭐를) | what |
| 어떻게 [어떠케] | how |
| 열심히 [열씨미] | hard/dilligently |
| 왜 | why |
| 요즘 | these days |
| 잘 | well |
| 좀 | a little |

## Memo

Lesson

# 5

# 가족이 어떻게 돼요?

(Tell me about your family.)

Lesson

# 5 가족이 어떻게 돼요? (Tell me about your family.)

말하기 1 가족이 어떻게 돼요? (Tell me about your family.)

말하기 2 친구하고 같이 테니스 쳐요. (I play tennis with a friend.)

말하기 3 커피숍에서 일해요. (I work at a coffee shop.)

말하기 4 이거 누구 책이에요? (Whose book is this?)

Upon completion of this lesson, you will be able to:

1. Discuss your family members
2. Describe your daily activities as they occur in a variety of places
3. Discuss people's belongings

**Grammatical items**

- 있으세요/계세요 (Honorific words)
- Vowel contractions
- 에서 (Locative particle for action verbs)
- 하고 같이 (With N)
- 의 (Possessive particle)
- N 것/거 (Possessive)

## 표현 (Expression) 집이 어디예요?

| | |
|---|---|
| **준** | 서리나, 집이 어디예요? |
| **서리나** | 네? 다시 한 번 말해 주세요. |
| **준** | 집이 어디예요? |
| **서리나** | 제 집*은 토론토예요. 준 집은 어디예요? (*제 집: my house) |
| **준** | 제 집은 서울이에요. |

| | |
|---|---|
| **집이 어디예요?**<br>**고향*이 어디예요?**<br>**(*고향: hometown)** | This expression may be used to ask about one's hometown or about a local residence. The above dialogue uses the expression to ask about one's hometown. But if the context uses the expression to ask about one's local residence, one can explain the place of his/her local residence as in the following example.<br>(e.g.) 제 집은 기숙사예요. 제 집은 다운타운이에요. |
| **다시 한번 말해 주세요.** | Please say that again. |

연습

Practice the following dialogue with your partner.

A (Name), 집이 어디예요?

B (Name), 다시 한번 말해 주세요.

A 집이 어디예요?

B 아, 제 집은 ________________ 이에요/예요. (Name) 집은 어디예요?

A 제 집은 ________________ 이에요/예요.

## 문화 (Culture)

One of the main characteristics of 한글 is familism and collectivism. Respect for the group, whether it be the country, family, school, society, neighbour, or hometown, has been fundamental in Korean society. Compared with Western culture, in which the individual is given more worth, Koreans consider their groups as a single entity, and this thinking has a huge impact on the way they behave and speak. One typical linguistic example of this phenomenon is '우리' (we, our). The word, 'my,' is mostly expressed as '우리' (we, our) in Korean, instead of '제' (my). The following are examples of '우리' which translate as 'my' in English.

| 우리 집 | 우리 나라 | 우리 가족 | 우리 남편 | 우리 아빠 |
|---|---|---|---|---|
| My house | My country | My family | My husband | My father |
| 우리 엄마 | 우리 학교 | 우리 선생님 | 우리 이웃 | 우리 동네 |
| My mother | My school | My teacher | My neighbour | My town |

## 발음 (Pronunciations)

### Aspiration of 'ㅎ'

When the consonant 'ㅎ' is combined with plain plosive consonants (ㄱ, ㄷ, ㅂ, ㅈ), they become the corresponding aspirated consonants.

| | ㄱ + ㅎ / ㅎ + ㄱ | ㄷ + ㅎ / ㅎ + ㄷ | ㅂ + ㅎ / ㅎ + ㅂ | ㅈ + ㅎ / ㅎ + ㅈ |
|---|---|---|---|---|
| **Aspiration** | ㅋ | ㅌ | ㅍ | ㅊ |
| **Examples** | 백화점 [배콰점]<br>좋고 [ ]<br>축하 [ ]<br>어떻게 [ ] | 많다 [ ]<br>않다 [ ] | 입학 [ ]<br>잡히다 [ ]<br>뽑히다 [ ] | 좋지 [ ]<br>쌓지 [ ] |

연습 1

**Practice reading the following sentences with your partner.**

1 저는 오늘 백화점에 가요.
2 커피도 좋고 주스도 좋아요.
3 생일을 축하해요.
4 요즘 어떻게 지내세요?
5 숙제가 많다.
6 음식이 좋지 않다.

## Palatalization

The [ㄷ] or [ㅌ] sound is palatalized when it comes together with the vowel [i] or the semivowel [y] (e.g. 이, 여).

| | palatalization | |
|---|---|---|
| ㄷ + [이, 여]. | [ㅈ] | 굳이 [구지], 맏이 [마지] |
| ㅌ + [이, 여]. | [ㅊ] | 붙여요 [부쳐요], 같이 [가치], 밑이 [미치] |

cf. 붙어요 [부터요], 같아요 [가타요], 밑에 [미테]

연습 2

**Practice reading the following sentences with your partner.**

1 우표를 붙여요. (I put a stamp on the letter.)
2 잘 붙어요. (It adheres well.)
3 책상 밑이 더러워요. (The bottom of the desk is dirty.)
4 책상 밑에 가방이 있어요. (There is a bag under the desk.)
5 이름이 같아요. (The names are the same.)
6 친구하고 같이 백화점에 가요. (I am going to the department store with a friend.)

Lesson 1 Lesson 2 Lesson 3 Lesson 4 Lesson 5 Lesson 6

## 말하기 (Speaking) 1. 가족이 어떻게 돼요?

**리아** 서리나는 가족이 어떻게 돼요?

**서리나** 아버지하고 어머니하고 언니하고 남동생이 있어요.

**리아** 부모님은 어디 계세요?

**서리나** 토론토에 계세요. 언니하고 동생도 토론토에 있어요. 저만 에드먼턴에 있어요.

**Leah** Tell me about your family.

**Cerina** I have a father, mother, older sister, and a younger brother in my family.

**Leah** Where are your parents?

**Cerina** They are in Toronto. My elder sister and my younger sibling are also in Toronto. I am the only person who is in Edmonton.

## 문법 (Grammar) ❶

### 1-1 Family members

In Korean, the names of family members change according to gender and family relations. For example, the suffix '외' is often added to mother-side family members (e.g. 외할아버지, 외사촌). And aunts are called differently based on which side they belongs to. Thus, aunts are called '고모' when they are related to father-side, and '이모' when they are related to mother-side.

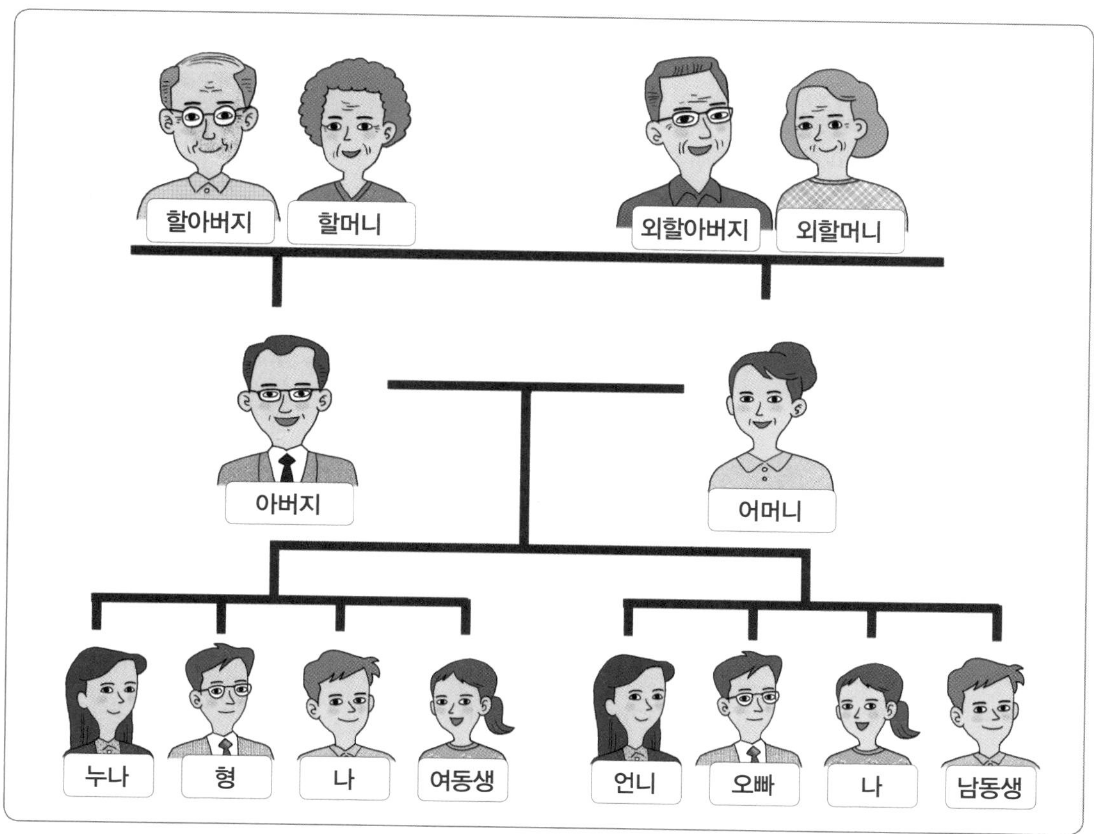


연습 1 Ask your partner about his/her family members as in the example.

A: (Name) 가족이 어떻게 돼요?

B: 저는 [ ] 하고 [ ] 이/가 있어요.

## 1-2 The particle '만'

The particle '만' means 'only' in English, and it is usually used after a noun.

(1) 서리나: 동생 있어요?

제니: 아니요, 없어요.

서리나: 언니는 있어요?

제니: 언니도 없어요. 오빠만 있어요.

| 서리나 | 샤닐 | 리아 |
|---|---|---|
| 캐나다 사람 | 캐나다 사람 | 한국 사람 |

(2) 서리나는 캐나다 사람이에요. 샤닐도 캐나다 사람이에요. 리아만 한국 사람이에요.

**연습 2** Interview your classmates and find a person who is different from the others in terms of school year and nationality. Make sentences using '만'.

| 이름 | | | |
|---|---|---|---|
| 학년 | | | |
| 나라 (nationality) | | | |

❶ ______________________.

❷ ______________________.

**연습 3** The following pictures show possession of items. Use the pictures to do a role play with your partner as in the example.

A: (Name), 사과 있어요?

B: 아니요, 없어요.

A: 그럼, 빵 있어요?

B: 아니요, 빵도 없어요. 바나나만 있어요.

| | 없어요 | 있어요 |
|---|---|---|
| 1 | 사과 빵 | 바나나 |

| 2 | 쿠키 | 햄버거 | 샌드위치 |
|---|---|---|---|
| 3 | 시계 | 컴퓨터 | 전화 |
| 4 | 피아노 | 하모니카 | 기타 |
| 5 | 개 | 토끼 | 고양이 |

## 1-3 '있으세요' / '계세요'

'있어요' has two honorific forms; '있으세요' and '계세요'. Thus, '있으세요' and '계세요' are used when the subject is a respected person. However, '있으세요' is used to talk about the respected person's possession of an item, while '계세요' is used to talk about the respected person's existence.

| | Existence | Possession |
|---|---|---|
| **Non-honorific** | 있어요 | 있어요 |
| **Honorific** | 계세요 | 있으세요 |

(1) 벤: 언니가 어디 있어요? (Where is your sister?)
서리나: 토론토에 있어요. (She is in Toronto.)
벤: 그럼, 부모님은 어디 계세요? (Then, where are your parents? Existence)
서리나: 부모님도 토론토에 계세요. (They are also in Toronto. Existence)

(2) 벤: 선생님, 여동생 있으세요? (Teacher, do you have a younger sister? Possession)
선생님: 네, 있어요. (Yes, I do.)
벤: 남동생도 있으세요? (Do you also have a younger brother? Possession)
선생님: 아니요, 없어요. (No I don't have.)

**연습 4** **Ask your partner the following questions.**

1. 여동생 (남동생, 오빠, 형) 있으세요?
2. 여동생 (남동생, 오빠, 형)은 어디 있어요?
3. 부모님은 어디 계세요?
4. 할아버지/할머니는 어디 계세요?

## 말하기 (Speaking) 2. 친구하고 같이 테니스 쳐요.

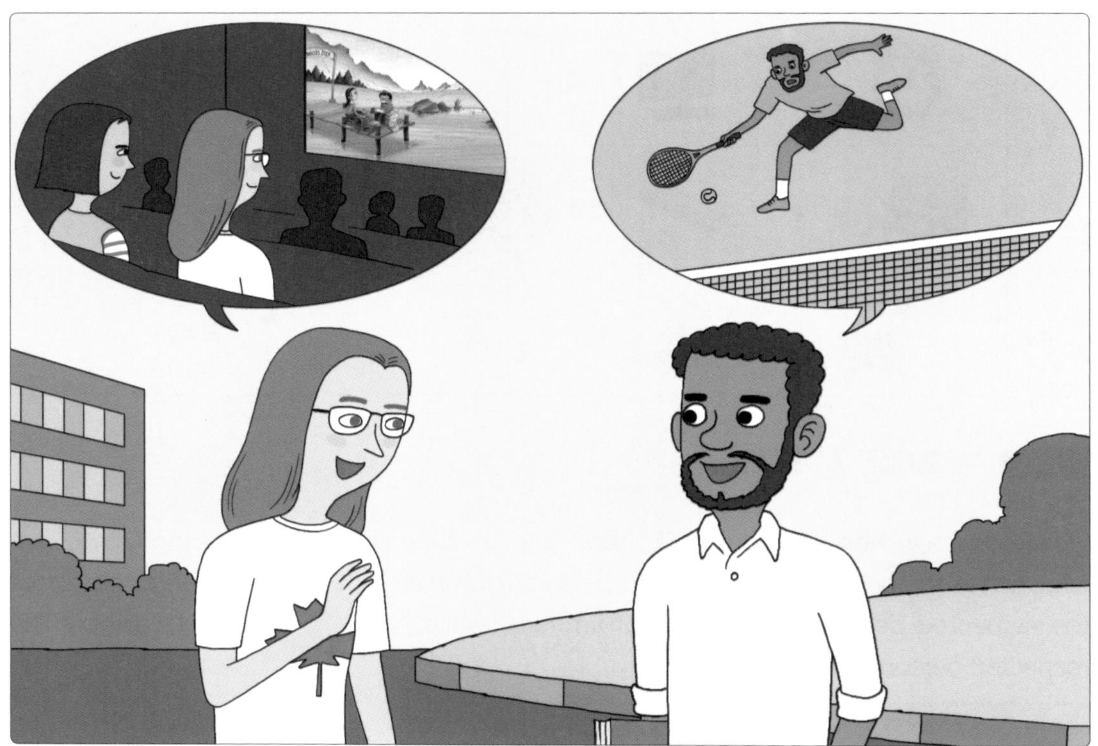

| | |
|---|---|
| 서리나 | 이번 주말에 뭐 해요? |
| 샤닐 | 아침에 형하고 같이 테니스 쳐요. 서리나는 이번 주말에 뭐 해요? |
| 서리나 | 저는 리아하고 같이 영화 봐요. |
| 샤닐 | 그래요? 저도 영화 좋아해요. 우리 영화관에 같이 가요. |
| 서리나 | 좋아요. |

| | |
|---|---|
| Cerina | What are you doing this weekend? |
| Shanil | I will play tennis with my older brother in the morning. What are you doing this weekend? |
| Cerina | I will watch a movie with Leah. |
| Shanil | Really? I like watching movies, too. Let's all go to the movie theater together. |
| Cerina | Okay. |

## 문법 (Grammar) ❷

### 2-1 Vowel contractions

Vowel contraction occurs when the last syllable of the stem does not have a final consonant.

**1.** When the stem has the vowel of '아', the two identical vowels become a single vowel.

| Dictionary ending | | Polite ending |
|---|---|---|
| 가다 | 가 + 아요 | 가요 |
| 타다 (to get a ride) | 타 + 아요 | 타요 |

자다 ______ 사다 ______

만나다 ______ 싸다 ______

비싸다 ______

Note: '하다' does not follow the above contraction rule, even if it has '아' vowel.

| 하다 | 하 + 여요 | 해요 |
|---|---|---|

공부하다 ______ 숙제하다 ______

**2.** When the stem has the vowel of '으', the vowel '으' is lost and the contraction occurs. Since the vowel '으' is lost, the vowel of the previous syllable decides the ending, '어요/아요'. Thus, as shown in (1), when the previous syllable has a bright vowel ('아' or '오'), the ending, '아요', is added to the stem. And, as shown in (2) when the previous syllable has a dark vowel ('어' or '예'), '어요' is added to the stem. However, as shown in (3), when there is no previous syllable, '어요' is the basic ending, like in '크다'.

| Dictionary ending | | Polite ending |
|---|---|---|
| (1) 나쁘다 | 나ㅃ + 아요 | 나빠요 |
| (2) 예쁘다 | 예ㅃ + 어요 | 예뻐요 |
| (3) 크다 | ㅋ + 어요 | 커요 |

바쁘다 ______ 예쁘다 ______

**3.** When the stem has the vowel '애', '어' from the ending '어요' is dropped.

| Dictionary ending | | Polite ending |
|---|---|---|
| 지내다 | 지내 + 어요 | 지내요 |

내다(to submit) [ ]

**4.** When the stem has the vowel '이', the vowel '이' is contracted with '어' of the ending '어요' and become '여'.

| Dictionary ending | | Polite ending |
|---|---|---|
| 마시다 | 마시 + 어요 | 마셔요 |

치다 [ ] 가르치다 [ ]

기다리다 [ ]

**5.** Honorific marker '시' is contracted into '세' when it is combined with the ending '어요'.

| Dictionary ending | | Polite ending |
|---|---|---|
| 안녕하시다 | 안녕하시 + 어요 | 안녕하세요 |

계시다 [ ]

cf. The syllable '시' in the word '마시다' is not an honorific marker; 마시다 → 마셔요. Thus, the honorific form of '마시다' is '마시세요' or '드세요'. And '드세요' is more commonly used in Korea.

**6.** When the vowel of the stem is '우' or '오', the contraction occurs into its diphthongs. '우' is a dark vowel and it is combined with '어요', while '오' is a bright vowel and it is combined with '아요'.

| Dictionary ending | | Polite ending |
|---|---|---|
| 주다 | 주 + 어요 | 줘요 |
| 오다 | 오 + 아요 | 와요 |

배우다 [ ] 보다 [ ]

However, when the preceding syllable has the first consonant, the contraction can be optional.

- 주다 → 주어요 or 줘요
- 보다 → 보아요 or 봐요

On the other hand, when the preceding syllable ends with '우' or '오', the contraction is obligatory.

- 오다 → 와요
- 배우다 → 배워요

**연습 1 Ask your partner the following questions, using the polite ending.**

매일 한국어 연습하다 → A: 매일 한국어 연습해요?
B: 네/ 아니요.

1. 보통 일찍* 자다. (*일찍: early)
2. (Name) 방이 크다
3. 요즘 잘 지내다
4. 매일 커피 마시다
5. 요즘 바쁘다
6. 매일 학교에 가다
7. 친구 생일에 선물을 주다
8. 요즘 한국어 배우다
9. 매일 텔레비전을 보다
10. 매일 도서관에 오다
11. 테니스 치다
12. 부모님이 캐나다에 계시다

## 2-2 '하고 (같이)'

'하고 같이' means 'together with someone' and it describes joint activities with someone. '같이' is optional but the particle '하고' is mandatory.

(1) 빵하고 주스를 먹어요. (하고: and)

(2) 샤닐: 벤, 내일 뭐 해요?
벤: 서리나하고* (같이) 테니스 쳐요. (*하고: With N)

**연습 2 Ask your partner the following questions. Use '-하고 같이' in your response as in the example.**

A: 오늘 뭐 해요?
B: 오늘 친구하고 같이 운동해요.

1. 오늘 뭐 해요?
2. 내일 뭐 해요?
3. 이번 주말에 뭐 해요?
4. 크리스마스에 뭐 해요?

## 2-3 Propositive informal sentence

Propositive sentences are used when making a suggestion. It means 'let's' in English. Propositive senences are made by adding '-어/아요' which is the same as the polite ending. Only verbs are used in making a propostive sentence.

(1) 서리나: 우리 언제 만나요? (When can we meet?)
    리아: 내일 만나요. (Let's meet tomorrow.)

(2) 서리나: 저는 오늘 요리해요. (Today I'm cooking.)
    리아: 그래요? 저하고 같이 해요. (Really? Let's do it together.)

**연습 3 Make dialogues with your partner using the propositive '어요/아요'.**

A: 오늘 뭐 해요?
B: 학교에 가요.
A: 그래요? 그럼, 저하고 같이 학교에 가요.

1. 오늘 뭐 해요?
2. 내일 어디 가요?
3. 이번 주말에 뭐 해요?
4. 심심해요*. (*심심해요: to be bored.)
5. 뭐 먹어요?
6. 뭐 마셔요?

## 말하기 (Speaking) 3. 커피숍에서 일해요.

| | |
|---|---|
| **줄리아** | 제니, 이번 주말에 어디 가요? |
| **제니** | 커피숍에 가요. |
| **줄리아** | 커피숍에서 친구 만나요? |
| **제니** | 아니요. 커피숍에서 일해요. 줄리아는 주말에 보통 뭐 해요? |
| **줄리아** | 저는 체육관에서 운동해요. |

| | |
|---|---|
| **Julia** | Jenny, where do you go on weekends? |
| **Jenny** | I go to a coffee shop. |
| **Julia** | Do you meet a friend at the coffee shop? |
| **Jenny** | No, I work at the coffee shop. What do you usually do on weekends? |
| **Julia** | I exercise at the gym. |

## 문법 (Grammar) ❸

### 3-1 The particle of the static location '에'

The locative particle '에' is used in referring to a static location which simply indicates the existence of an item or a person.

• Location에 + the predicate indicating the existence (있어요, 계세요)

(1) 벤: 학교 식당이 어디 있어요? (Where is the school cafeteria?)
서리나: 저 건물에 있어요. (It is in that building.)
(2) 벤: 서리나, 한국어 책이 어디 있어요? (Where is the Korean book?)
서리나: 제 가방 안에 있어요. (It is in my bag.)
(3) 벤: 부모님이 어디 계세요? (Where are your parents?)
서리나: 토론토에 계세요. (They are in Toronto.)

**연습 1** Ask your partner the following questions.

❶ 학교 식당이 어디 있어요?
❷ 한국어 책이 어디 있어요?
❸ 부모님이 어디 계세요?

### 3-2 The locative particle for the destination '에'

The locative particle '에' is used in referring to a destination or a goal.

• Location에 + Directional verb (가다, 오다)

(1) 서리나: 벤, 어디 가요? (Where are you going?)
벤: 우체국에 가요. 서리나는 어디 가요? (I'm going to the post office. Where are you going?)
서리나: 저는 백화점에 가요. (I'm going to the department store.)
(2) 서리나: 내일 학교에 와요? (Are you coming to school tomorrow?)
벤: 네, 내일 시험이 있어요. (Yes, I have an exam tomorrow.)
(3) 유미: 어디에 전화하세요? (Where are you calling?)
벤: 집에 전화해요. (I'm calling home.)
리아: 한국에 전화해요. (I'm calling someone in Korea.)

**연습 2** Ask your partner about where he/she is going, according to the pictures.

(Example) A: 지금 어디 가요?
B: 학교에 가요.

**연습 3** Find where the people are going. See the online appendix.

## 3-3 The locative particle for a dynamic activity '에서'

The particle '에서' is used in referring to location for a dynamic activity.

- Location에서 + verb describing actions (e.g. 운동하다, 사다, 공부하다, 먹다, 자다)

(1) 벤: 보통 어디(에)서 운동해요? (Where do you usually exercise?)
 줄리아: 체육관에서 운동해요. (I exercise at the gym.)

(2) 벤: 생일 선물을 어디서 사요? (Where do you buy the birthday gift?)
 제니: 백화점에서 사요. (I buy it at the department store.)

**연습 4** Ask your partner about where he/she is doing a certain activity, according to the picture.

A: 어디서 점심 먹어요?
B: 학교 식당에서 먹어요.

| (점심 먹다/학교 식당) | (기다리다/백화점 앞) | (일하다/커피숍) |
|---|---|---|
| (책을 읽다/서점) | (운동하다/체육관) | (영화를 보다/영화관) |

**연습 5** Ask your partner the following questions.

1. 요즘 어디서 공부해요?
2. 지금 어디 가요?
3. 한국어 교실은 어디 있어요?
4. 도서관은 어디 있어요?
5. 어디서 점심 먹어요?
6. 오늘 누구하고 점심 먹어요?
7. 어디서 커피 마셔요?
8. 어디서 친구를 만나요?
9. 어디서 숙제해요?
10. 어디에 전화해요?
11. 요즘 어디서 쇼핑해요?
12. 요즘 어디서 운동해요?

## 4. 이거 누구의 책이에요?

준 이거 누구 책이에요?
줄리아 제 책이에요.
준 그럼, 이건 누구 연필이에요?
줄리아 그건 선생님 거예요.

Jun Whose book is this?
Julia It's my book.
Jun Then, whose pencil is this?
Julia It's the teacher's.

## 문법 (Grammar) ④

### 4-1 Possessive particle '의'

The possessive particle '의' comes between the possessor and the possessed. The particle '의' is pronounced as [에]. In casual speech form, the possessive particle '의' is often omitted.

- 서리나의 책 (Possessor 의 Possessed) → 서리나 책 (Cerina's book)
- 오늘의 숙제 → 오늘 숙제 (Today's homework)
- 나의 어머니 → 내 어머니, 나의 이름 → 내 이름
- 저의 아버지 → 제 아버지, 저의 이름 → 제 이름, 우리 가족 → 저희 가족

(1) 벤: 이거 누구(의) 책이에요? (Whose book is this?)
서리나: 제니 책이에요. (It's Jenny's book.)
벤: 저건 누구 가방이에요? (Whose bag is that?)
서리나: 제 가방이에요. (It's my bag.)

**연습 1** Talk with your partner about who owns the items near you.

A: 이거 누구 [　　　] 이에요/예요?

B: [　　　] 이에요/예요.

A: 그럼, 그건 누구 [　　　] 이에요/예요?

B: [　　　] 이에요/예요.

### 4-12 '것/거' (thing or stuff)

'것/거' literally means 'thing', or 'stuff'. When the possessed object is obvious from the preceding context, '것/거' may replace the object. '거' is the contracted form of '것'. '거' is used in casual speech and '것' is used in writing or in formal situations.

(1) 서리나: 이거 누구 책이에요? (Whose book is this?)
벤: 제 거예요. (It's mine. Instead of '제 책이에요'.) (Cerina shows another book to Ben.)
서리나: 그럼, 그건 누구 거예요? (Then, whose book is that?)
벤: 아, 그건 선생님 거예요. (Ah, it's the teacher's.)

**연습 2** Pair work

Explain about who owns the items in the picture.

A: 이거 누구 지갑이에요?

B: 서리나 거예요.

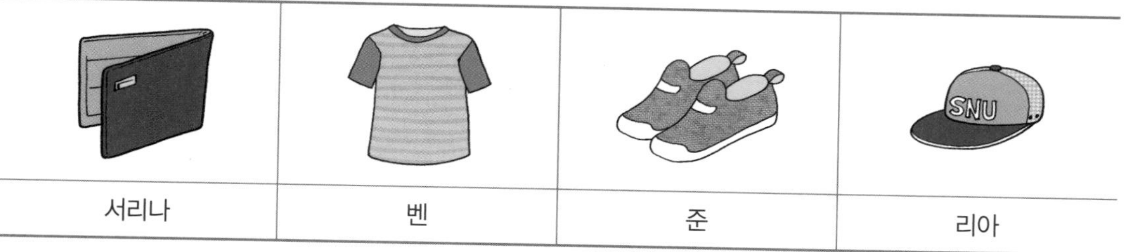


| 서리나 | 벤 | 준 | 리아 |
|---|---|---|---|

**연습 3** Practice the following dialogue with your partner, using the pictures.

A: 이거 누구 가방이에요? (Name) 거예요?

B: 아니요. 우리 언니/형/오빠/동생 거예요.

A: (Name) 거는 어디 있어요?

B: 제 거는 집에 있어요.

| 언니/누나 | 형/오빠 | 남동생 | 여동생 |
|---|---|---|---|
| 어머니 | 아버지 | 샤닐 | 벤 |
| 서리나 | 리아 | 친구 | 선생님 |

## 읽기 (Reading) 1. 주말에 부모님이 오세요.

| | |
|---|---|
| **리아** | 서리나, 이 선물 누구 거예요? |
| **서리나** | 제 부모님 거예요. 내일 부모님이 우리 기숙사에 오세요. |
| **리아** | 그래요? 부모님은 지금 어디 계세요? |
| **서리나** | 토론토에 계세요. |
| **리아** | 서리나는 형제가 있어요? |
| **서리나** | 네, 언니하고 남동생이 있어요. 리아도 언니가 있어요? |
| **리아** | 아니요, 저는 오빠만 있어요. 그런데 서리나는 오늘 저녁에 뭐 해요? |
| **서리나** | 한국 음식을 요리해요. |
| **리아** | 그래요? 그럼, 저하고 같이 해요. |
| **서리나** | 네, 좋아요. |

## 읽기 (Reading) 2. 서리나의 가족

서리나의 가족은 아버지하고 어머니하고 언니하고 남동생이 있어요.
서리나 부모님은 토론토에 계세요. 서리나의 언니하고 동생도 토론토에 있어요.
서리나 아버지는 학교에서 영어를 가르치세요. 서리나 어머니는 도서관에서 일하세요.
언니는 대학원생이에요. 그리고 음악을 전공해요. 서리나는 언니하고 사이가 좋아요.
그래서 매일 전화해요. 서리나의 남동생은 고등학생이에요.
주말에 보통 남동생은 친구하고 같이 공원에서 운동해요.
그런데 이번 주말에 서리나 부모님이 기숙사에 오세요. 그래서 서리나는 오늘 백화점에 가요.
백화점에서 부모님 선물을 사요 . 그리고 저녁에 리아하고 같이 한국 음식을 요리해요.

**연습 1** Read the narration and respond to the following questions.

1. 서리나 가족은 어떻게 돼요?
2. 서리나 부모님은 어디 계세요?
3. 서리나 어머니는 어디서 일하세요?
4. 서리나는 오늘 뭐 해요?
5. 서리나는 오늘 누구 선물을 사요?
6. 누가 대학원에서 음악을 공부해요?

**연습 2** Write to describe your family.

1. Introduce your family members.

2. Describe each family member.

3. Where are your family members?

4. Who are you close to in your family?

5. What do your parents do on weekends?

## 읽기 (Reading) 1. My parents are coming this weekend.

**Leah** Cerina, who is this present for?

**Cerina** It's for my parents.

**Leah** Really? Where are your parents now?

**Cerina** They are in Toronto.

**Leah** Do you have any sibling?

**Cerina** Yes, I have a sister and a younger brother. Do you have a sister, too?

**Leah** No, I have only a brother. By the way, what are you doing now?

**Cerina** I am cooking Korean food.

**Leah** Really? Then, let's do it toegether.

**Cerina** Okay. It's great.

## 읽기 (Reading) 2. Cerina's family

Cerina has a father, mother, sister, and brother in her family. Cerina's parents are in Toronto. Cerina's sister and her younger brother are also in Toronto. Cerina's father teaches English at school. Cerina's mother works at a library. Cerina's sister is a graduate student, majoring in music. Cerina and her sister have a good relationship. So they talk on the phone every day. Cerina's younger brother is a high school student. He usually exercises with his friends at the park on weekends. This weekend, Cerina's parents are coming to visit her dormitory. So Cerina is buying a present for them at the department store. And, in the evening, she cooks Korean food with Leah.

## 어휘 Vocabulary

### Nouns

| | |
|---|---|
| 가게 | store |
| 가족 | family |
| 건물 | building |
| 고등학생 [고등학쌩] | high school student |
| 공원 | park |
| 남동생 | younger brother |
| 누나 | the older sister of a male |
| 대학원생 [대하권생] | graduate student |
| 동생 | younger sibling |
| 백화점 [배콰점] | department store |
| 부모님 | parents |
| 사이 | relationship |
| 생일 | birthday |
| 선물 | present, gift |
| 아버지 | father |
| 어머니 | mother |
| 언니 | the older sister of a female |
| 여동생 | younger sister |
| 영화관 | movie theatre |
| 오빠 | the older brother of a female |
| 우리 | we |
| 저녁 | supper, evening |
| 점심 | lunch |
| 주말 | weekend |
| 체육관 [체육꽌] | gym |
| 친척 | relative |
| 커피숍 | coffee shop |
| 테니스 | tennis |
| 할아버지 [하라버지] | grandfather |
| 할머니 | grandmother |
| 형 | the older brother of a male |
| 형제 | siblings |

### Verbs

| | |
|---|---|
| 계시다 | to be (existence) |
| 기다리다 | to wait |
| 되다 | to become |
| 배우다 | to learn |
| 보다 | to see, look, watch |
| 사다 | to buy |
| 쇼핑(하다) | to shop |
| 연습하다 [연스파다] | to practice |
| 오다 | to come |
| 요리(하다) | to cook |
| 운동(하다) | to exercise |
| 일(하다) | to work |
| 주다 | to give |
| 치다 | to play (tennis) |

### Adjectives

| | |
|---|---|
| 비싸다 | to be expensive |

### Other expressions

| | |
|---|---|
| 같이 [가치] | together |
| 다시 | again |
| 만 | only |
| 매일 | every day |
| 보통 | usually |
| 이번 | this time |
| 한 번 | one time (frequency) |

LIBRARY

Lesson

# 6

# 지금 몇 시예요?

(What time is it?)

Lesson

# 6 지금 몇 시예요? (What time is it?)

말하기 1 전화 번호가 뭐예요? (What's your phone number?)

말하기 2 사과 두 개 주세요. (Please give me two apples.)

말하기 3 지금 몇 시예요? (What time is it now?)

말하기 4 선물 사러 백화점에 가요. (I am going to the department store to buy a gift.)

Upon completion of this lesson, you will be able to:

1. Use numbers correctly according to the situation
2. Explain the purpose of coming or going to a place

**Grammatical items**

- Numbers
- Counter markers
- Reading time
- Irregular verb in ㄷ
- 요일 (Days)
- –(으)러 가요/와요
  (Expression to describe a purpose)

## 표현 (Expression) 오래간만이에요.

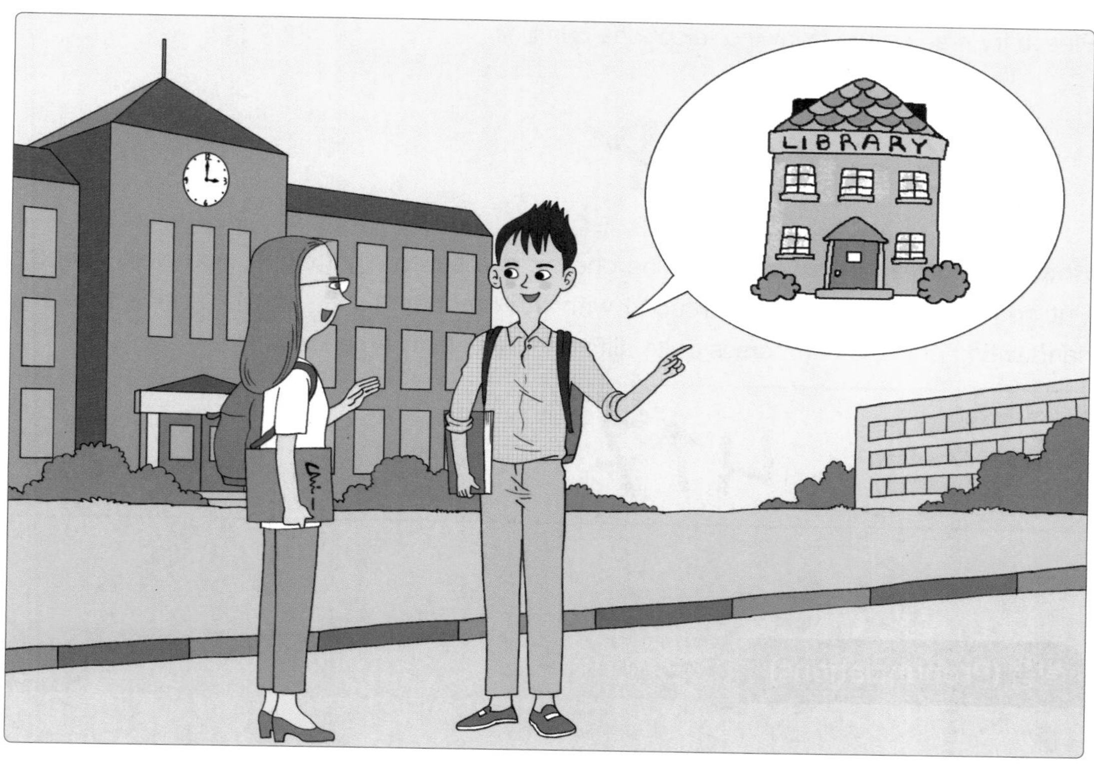


**서리나** 케빈, 오래간만이에요.

**케빈** 네, 오래간만이에요. 요즘 어떻게 지내요?

**서리나** 잘 지내요. 지금 어디 가요?

**케빈** 지금 도서관에 가요. 내일 시험이 있어요.

**서리나** 그래요? 그럼, 나중에 봐요.

| | |
|---|---|
| **오래간만이에요.** | It is used when two people meet after a long while. It means 'Long time no see' in English. |
| **나중에 봐요** | See you later. |

## 문화 (Culture)

Please try reading the following telephone number.

916-1788

How did you read it? If you read 'nine one six one seven eight eight', you were correct. But some of you might be confused with the number '1','7', and '9', since Koreans handwriting of these numbers is quite different from North Americans.

| North American | 417 | Korean | 417 |
|---|---|---|---|

## 발음 (Pronunciations) Review

1. 'ㅎ' Aspiration: 몇 학년 ______

2. Nasalization: 몇 명 ______, 몇 마리 ______

3. The pronunciation of numbers

11 ______, 12 ______, 16 ______

Note: For the number '16', 'ㄴ' sound is inserted, and then nasalization occurs.

'십육' [십뉵] → [심뉵]

## 말하기 (Speaking) 1. 전화번호가 뭐예요?

| | |
|---|---|
| **제니** | 벤은 집이 어디예요? |
| **벤** | 제 집은 학교 옆 아파트예요. |
| **제니** | 집 전화번호는 뭐예요? |
| **벤** | 780-432-5678이에요. |

| | |
|---|---|
| **Jenny** | Where is your home? |
| **Ben** | I live in an apartment beside the school. |
| **Jenny** | What's your phone number? |
| **Ben** | It's 780-432-5678. |

Lesson 1 Lesson 2 Lesson 3 Lesson 4 Lesson 5 Lesson 6

## 문법 (Grammar) ❶

### 1-1 Sino-Korean numbers '0-10'

Sino-Korean numbers are used to refer to specific numbers relating to money, telephone numbers, class numbers, house numbers, etc., while native Korean numbers are used to count small numbers of people or items such as apples, chairs, rooms, etc.

| 0 | 1 | 2 | 3 | 4 | 5 | 6 | 7 | 8 | 9 | 10 |
|---|---|---|---|---|---|---|---|---|---|---|
| 영/공 | 일 | 이 | 삼 | 사 | 오 | 육 | 칠 | 팔 | 구 | 십 |

The question word '몇' (What, how many) is used with the counter, such as '몇 학년', '몇 번', '몇 개', '몇 마리', '몇 명'. In addition, in saying the telephone numbers, '공' is used instead of '영,' and the dash symbol is read as '에'. For example, the phone number of 780-432-5678 is read as '칠팔공에 사삼이에 오육칠팔'.

(1) 줄리아: 벤은 몇 학년이에요? (What year are you in?)
 벤: 일학년이에요. (I'm in my first year.)

(2) 줄리아: 전화 번호가 뭐예요? (What is your phone number?)
 벤: 780-432-5678이에요. (It is 780-432-5678.)

**연습 1** Practice the following dialogue with your partner, using the given phone numbers.

A: 집 전화 번호가 뭐예요?
B: 475-7829예요.

| 475-7829 | 732-6908 | 493-6503 | 308-3826 |
|---|---|---|---|
| 239-0517 | 780-3479 | 271-6349 | 874-9035 |

**연습 2** Ask your classmates' phone numbers. Listen and write the numbers.

| 이름 | 전화번호 | 이름 | 전화번호 |
|---|---|---|---|
| | | | |
| | | | |
| | | | |
| | | | |

## 1-2 Sino Korean numbers '1 – 100'

| 1 | 2 | 3 | 4 | 5 | 6 | 7 | 8 | 9 | 10 |
|---|---|---|---|---|---|---|---|---|---|
| 일 | 이 | 삼 | 사 | 오 | 육 | 칠 | 팔 | 구 | 십 |
| 11 | 12 | 13 | 14 | 15 | 16 | 17 | 18 | 19 | 20 |
| 십일 | 십이 | 십삼 | 십사 | 십오 | 십육 | 십칠 | 십팔 | 십구 | 이십 |

| 10 | 20 | 30 | 40 | 50 | 60 | 70 | 80 | 90 | 100 |
|---|---|---|---|---|---|---|---|---|---|
| 십 | 이십 | 삼십 | 사십 | 오십 | 육십 | 칠십 | 팔십 | 구십 | 백 |

| 100 | 1,000 | 10,000 |
|---|---|---|
| 백 | 천 | 만 |

When referring to a specific amount of money, Sino-Korean numbers are used. For example, '1000원' is read as '천 원' (approximately 1달러), and '10달러' is read as '십 달러' (approximately '만 원').

100원 = 백 원
(around 10 cents)

500원 = 오백 원
(around 50 cents)

1000원 = 천 원
(around 1 dollar)

5000원 = 오천 원
(around 5 dollars)

10,000원 = 만 원
(around 10 dollars)

**연습 3** Practice the Sino-Korean numbers with the number cards in the online appendix.

**연습 4** Role play: Take turns for role playing an employee and a customer. Make dialogues as in the example.

A: 햄버거 있어요?
B: 네, 있어요.
A: 얼마예요? (How much is it?)
B: 6,700원이에요.

|  |  |  |  |  |  |
|---|---|---|---|---|---|
|  | 케이크<br>28,000원 |  | 햄버거<br>6,700원 |  | 라면<br>2,900원 |
|  | 껌<br>500원 |  | 아이스크림<br>1,300원 |  | 주스<br>1,670원 |
|  | 우유<br>2,300원 |  | 김밥<br>3,200원 |  | 비빔밥<br>8,000원 |
|  | 치킨<br>5,500원 |  | 커피<br>4,500원 |  | 과자<br>730원 |

**연습 5** **Market Game. (See the materials in the online appendix) In groups, decide your roles as buyers or sellers.**

(1) Buyers: Ask for an item. (e.g. 가방 있어요?)
(2) Sellers: Tell the price of the item. (e.g. 네, 3,500원이에요.)
(3) Buyers: Write down the price you hear. (e.g. 네, 3,500원이에요.)
(4) If the written number or price the buyers write down is correct, they get to keep the item.

## 말하기 (Speaking) 2. 사과 두 개 주세요.

서리나 사과 있어요?
가게 주인* 네, 있어요.
서리나 사과 두 개 주세요.
가게 주인* 네, 3달러예요.

Cerina Do you have any apples?
Seller Yes, we do.
Cerina Please give me two apples.
Seller Sure. That's 3 dollars.

* 가게 주인: the shop owner

## 문법 (Grammar) ❷

### 2-1 Native Korean Numbers

Native Korean numbers are used to counting small numbers of items, such as apples, chairs, rooms, or people, etc. When referring to the age, the native Korean numbers are also used. '살' is the counter which is attached to the number of a particular age.

| 1 | 하나 | 한 살 | 11 | 열 하나 | 열 한 살 | 21 | 스물 하나 | 스물 한 살 |
|---|---|---|---|---|---|---|---|---|
| 2 | 둘 | 두 살 | 12 | 열 둘 | 열 두 살 | 22 | 스물 둘 | 스물 두 살 |
| 3 | 셋 | 세 살 | 13 | 열 셋 | 열 세 살 | 23 | 스물 셋 | 스물 세 살 |
| 4 | 넷 | 네 살 | 14 | 열 넷 | 열 네 살 | 24 | 스물 넷 | 스물 네 살 |
| 5 | 다섯 | 다섯 살 | 15 | 열 다섯 | 열 다섯 살 | 25 | 스물 다섯 | 스물 다섯 살 |
| 6 | 여섯 | 여섯 살 | 16 | 열 여섯 | 열 여섯 살 | 26 | 스물 여섯 | 스물 여섯 살 |
| 7 | 일곱 | 일곱 살 | 17 | 열 일곱 | 열 일곱 살 | 27 | 스물 일곱 | 스물 일곱 살 |
| 8 | 여덟 | 여덟 살 | 18 | 열 여덟 | 열 여덟 살 | 28 | 스물 여덟 | 스물 여덟 살 |
| 9 | 아홉 | 아홉 살 | 19 | 열 아홉 | 열 아홉 살 | 29 | 스물 아홉 | 스물 아홉 살 |
| 10 | 열 | 열 살 | 20 | 스물 | 스무 살 | 30 | 서른 | 서른 살 |

| 10 | 20 | 30 | 40 | 50 | 60 | 70 | 80 | 90 | 100 |
|---|---|---|---|---|---|---|---|---|---|
| 열 | 스물 | 서른 | 마흔 | 쉰 | 예순 | 일흔 | 여든 | 아흔 | 백 |

(1) 서리나: 벤 형은 몇 살이에요? (How old is Ben's brother?)
벤: 25살이에요. (He is 25 years old.)

#### 연습 1 Ask your classmates their ages.

| 이름 | 나이 (age) | 이름 | 나이 (age) |
|---|---|---|---|
| | | | |
| | | | |
| | | | |
| | | | |

## 2-2 Native Korean Number + Counter

보기 '한 명' (person), '두 사람' (person), '세 개' (item), '네 마리' (animal), '다섯 권' (book)

In Korean, native Korean numbers are used to count some objects and followed by counters as in the example above. The counter is a noun that is associated with a number in counting objects. '명', '사람', '개', '마리', and '권' are the examples of the counters as shown above. In English concept, it is similar to a counting unit such as 'glass' in 'a glass of water'.

The followings are the examples of the counters that come with native numbers.

몇 개예요?
몇 사람이에요?
몇 명이에요?
몇 권이에요?
몇 마리예요?
몇 시간이에요?
6 hours
몇 시예요?


(2) 저는 매일 여덟 시간 자요. (I sleep for eight hours every day.)

(3) 리아: 한국어 수업은 몇 시간이에요? (How long is the Korean class?)
서리나: 두 시간이에요. (It is two hours long.)

## 2-3 Sino-Korean number + Counter

Sion-Korean numbers are used mostly when referring to a specific number.

For example, '학년' (the specific school year), '층' (the specific floor), '과' (the specific chapter), '년' (the specific year), '월' (the specific month), '일' (the specific date), '달러' (Canadian currency), and '원' (Korean currency) come with sino-Korean numbers. Sino-Korean numbers are also used when you count a larger number of people or items. (Example) 45명

| 몇 학년이에요? |  | 몇 월이에요? |  | 며칠이에요?<br>(몇 일 → 며칠) | 26TH |
|---|---|---|---|---|---|

| 몇 층이에요? | 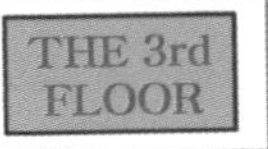  | 몇 년이에요? |   | 몇 과예요? |   |
|---|---|---|---|---|---|

(4) 저는 2학년이에요. (I am a second year student.)
(5) 한국어 교실은 3층에 있어요. (The Korean class is on the 3rd floor.)
(6) 지금 4과 공부해요. (We are studying Lesson 4 now.)
(7) 2021년에 만나요. (Let's meet in 2021.)
(8) 5월은 방학이에요. (방학: vacation, We have vacation in May.)
  cf. '달' uses native Korean numbers, while '월' uses sino-Korean numbers.
    (한 달, 두 달, 세 달 vs 일 월, 이 월, 삼 월)
(9) 25일이 제 생일이에요. (The 25th is my birthday.)
(10) 냉장고가 890달러예요. (The refrigerator is 890 dollars.)
(11) 필통이 2,500원이에요. (The pencil case is 2500 won.)
(12) 교실에 학생이 45명 있어요. (There are 45 students in the classroom.)

**연습 2** Practice with using the counter cards in the online appendix with your partner.

**연습 3** Ask your partner about the numbers in the following pictures, as in the example.

(Example) A: 몇 시간이에요? B: 여섯 시간이에요.

| ❶ 6 hours | ❷ | ❸ | ❹ sep 20 | ❺ 2019 |
|---|---|---|---|---|
| ❻ | ❼ the 2nd year | ❽ | ❾ 2 과 | ❿ |
| ⓫ November | ⓬ | ⓭ The 3rd floor | | |

## 2-4 Word order with counters

• Noun (particle) + Number + Counter

A proper particle is added to the noun, according to the grammatical role of the noun in the sentence.

| | | | | | |
|---|---|---|---|---|---|
| • 오빠 (가) | 두 | 명 | • 가방 (이) | 세 | 개 |
| • 책 (이) | 네 | 권 | • 강아지 (가) | 한 | 마리 |
| • 침대 (가) | 다섯 | 개 | | | |

(1) 리아는 오빠가 2명 있어요. or 리아는 오빠 2명이 있어요. (Leah has two brothers.)
(2) 저는 가방이 3개 있어요. or 저는 가방 3개가 있어요. (I have three bags.)
(3) 저는 오늘 책을 2권 읽어요. or 저는 오늘 책 2권을 읽어요. (I read two books today.)

**연습 4** **Ask the following questions to your partner.**

1. 우리 교실에 학생이 몇 명 있어요?
2. 지금 우리는 한국어 몇 과 공부해요?
3. 우리 교실이 몇 층에 있어요?
4. 집에 방이 몇 개 있어요?
5. 집에 문이 몇 개 있어요?
6. 매일 한국어를 몇 시간 공부해요?
7. 강아지 있어요? 몇 마리 있어요?
8. 가방이 몇 개 있어요?
9. 가방에 책이 몇 권 있어요?
10. 가족이 몇 명이에요?

## 말하기 (Speaking) 3. 지금 몇 시예요?

| | |
|---|---|
| 벤 | 지금 몇 시예요? |
| 샤닐 | 오전 11시 10분이에요. |
| 벤 | 학교에 보통 몇 시에 와요? |
| 샤닐 | 오전 9시에 와요. |
| 벤 | 점심은 보통 몇 시에 먹어요? |
| 샤닐 | 오후 12시 30분에 먹어요. |

| | |
|---|---|
| Ben | What time is it now? |
| Shanil | It’s 11:10 a.m. |
| Ben | What time do you usually come to school? |
| Shanil | I come at 9 a.m. |
| Ben | At what time do you usually have lunch? |
| Shanil | I usually eat it at 12:30. |

## 문법 (Grammar) ❸

### 3-1 Reading time

- '시' (Hour): Native Korean numbers
- '분' (Minutes): Sino-Korean numbers

(Example) 12시 50분 – 열두 시 오십 분
8시 30분 – 여덟 시 삼십 분 or 여덟 시 반

More time-related expressions

| | | |
|---|---|---|
| 아침<br>오전 | | 7am - 9 am |
| | | 10am - 11am |
| 낮 | 정오 | 12 pm, Noon |
| | 오후 | 1 pm - 5 pm |
| 저녁 | | 6 pm - 8 pm |
| 밤 | | 9 pm - 1 am |

The time particle 에 is added after the time in a sentence.
(1) 벤은 8시에 아침을 먹어요. (Ben eats breakfast at 8 o'clock in the morning.)
(2) 벤은 오전 10시에 학교에 가요. (Ben goes to school at 10 am.)

**연습 1** Practice reading the times on the clocks with your partner.

A: 몇 시예요?
B: ______시 ______분이에요.

**연습 2** Ask the following questions to your partner.

1. 한국어 수업은 몇 시에 있어요?
2. 몇 시에 아침을 먹어요?
3. 몇 시에 학교에 가요?
4. 몇 시에 집에 가요?
5. 몇 시에 점심을 먹어요?
6. 몇 시에 저녁을 먹어요?
7. 몇 시에 자요?
8. 몇 시에 텔레비전을 봐요?
9. 몇 시에 친구를 만나요?
10. 몇 시에 숙제해요?

**연습 3** Interview your partner about their favorite TV programs.

| 이름이 뭐예요? | TV에서 뭘 봐요? | 몇 시에 봐요? | 프로그램이 몇 시간 해요? |
|---|---|---|---|
| | | | |
| | | | |
| | | | |

## 말하기 (Speaking) 4. 선물 사러 백화점에 가요.

| | |
|---|---|
| **벤** | 서리나, 어디 가요? |
| **서리나** | 수업 들으러 학교에 가요. 벤은 어디 가요? |
| **벤** | 저는 생일 선물 사러 백화점에 가요. |
| **서리나** | 누구 생일이에요? |
| **벤** | 이번 토요일이 제 형 생일이에요. |

| | |
|---|---|
| **Ben** | Cerina, where are you going? |
| **Cerina** | I am going to school to take a class. Where are you going? |
| **Ben** | I am going to the department store to buy a birthday gift. |
| **Cerina** | Whose birthday is it? |
| **Ben** | This Saturday is my older brother's birthday. |

## 문법 (Grammar) ❹

### 4-1 Days of the week

| 월요일 | 화요일 | 수요일 | 목요일 | 금요일 | 토요일 | 일요일 |
|---|---|---|---|---|---|---|
| Monday | Tuesday | Wednesday | Thursday | Friday | Saturday | Sunday |

**연습 1** Look at the suggested information and ask your partner about where he/she goes and what he/she does on a particular day.

A: 월요일에 어디 가세요? / 뭐 먹어요?
B: 한국어 교실에 가요. / 햄버거 먹어요.

어디 가세요?

뭐 먹어요?

토요일 월요일 수요일 일요일 금요일 목요일 화요일

- Monday: 한국어 교실에 가요
- Tuseday: 커피숍에 가요
- Wednesday: 백화점에 가요
- Thursday: 도서관에 가요
- Friday: 노래방에 가요
- Saturday: 파티에 가요
- Sunday: 친구 집에 가요

- Monday: 햄버거* 먹어요
- Tuesday: 스파게티* 먹어요
- Wednesday: 피자* 먹어요
- Thursday: 김밥* 먹어요
- Friday: 라면* 먹어요
- Saturday: 떡볶이* 먹어요
- Sunday: 불고기* 먹어요

*햄버거: hamburger, 스파게티: spaghetti, 피자: pizza, 김밥: kimbap, 라면: instant noodles, 불고기: bulgogi

**연습 2** Interview your partner with the following questions.

| 친구 이름 | 월요일에 어디 가요? |
|---|---|
| 화요일에 어디 가요? | 수요일에 뭐 해요? |
| 목요일에 뭐 해요? | 금요일에 뭐 해요? |
| 토요일에 뭐 먹어요? | 일요일에 뭐 먹어요? |

## 4-1 The irregular predicate in 'ㄷ'

When the stem of a particular predicate has 'ㄷ' as final, 'ㄷ' changes into 'ㄹ' before a vowel.

- 듣다 → 들어요 (듣 + 어요 → 들어요)
- 듣다 → 들으세요 (듣 + 으세요 → 들으세요)

- 걷다 → 걸어요 (걷 + 어요 → 걸어요)
- 걷다 → 걸으세요 (걷 + 으세요 → 걸으세요)

(1) 벤: 서리나, 일요일에 보통 뭐 해요? (Cerina, what do you usually do on Sunday?)
서리나: 공원에서 걸어요. (I walk in the park.)

(2) 서리나: 벤, 방에서 뭐 해요? (Ben, what do you do in your room?)
벤: 음악을 들어요. (I listen to music.)

(3) 서리나: 벤, 아침에 보통 뭐 해요? (Ben, what do you usually do in the morning?)
벤: 라디오를 들어요. (I listen to the radio.)

(4) 서리나: 이번 학기에 뭐 들어요? (What do you take this semester?)
벤: 경제학 들어요. (I take Economics.)
서리나: 이번 학기에 몇 과목 들어요? (How many courses do you take this semester?)
벤: 네 과목 들어요. (I take four courses.)

**연습 3** Ask the following questions to your partner.

1. 이번 학기에 뭐 들어요?
2. 이번 학기에 몇 과목 들어요?
3. 보통 언제 음악 들어요?
4. 보통 어디에서 음악을 들어요?
5. 보통 어디에서 걸어요?

## 4-1 '-(으)러'

'-(으)러' is used to indicate the purpose of going or coming to a particular place.
When verb stem has a final consonant, it takes '으러'. (먹다 → 먹으러)
When a verb stem has no final, it takes '러'. (사다 → 사러)

(1) 서리나: 벤, 지금 어디 가요? (Ben, where are you going now?)
벤: 백화점에 가요. (I am going to the department store.)
서리나: 왜요? (Why?)
벤: 신발 사러 (백화점에) 가요. (I am going there to buy shoes.)

**연습 4** Look at the picture and describe the purpose of the action.

A: 어디 가요?

B: 점심 먹으러 학교 식당에 가요.

**연습 5** Describe your possible purpose of going to each of the suggested places.

A: 어디 가요?

B: 커피 마시러 커피숍에 가요.

| Purpose | Place |
|---|---|
| 공부하다, 먹다, 만나다, 사다, 숙제하다, 보다, 마시다, 자다, 읽다, 듣다, 가르치다, 운동하다, 연습하다, 전화하다, 노래하다 | 커피숍, 친구 집, 백화점, 가게, 서점, 헬스장, 집, 학교, 우체국, 영화관, 한국, 노래방 |

**연습 6** Interview your partner about where they go on a particular day, and why they go there.

A: 월요일에 어디 가요?

B: 학교에 가요.

A: 왜 학교에 가요?

B: 수업 들으러 학교에 가요.

| | 월요일 | 화요일 | 수요일 | 목요일 | 금요일 | 토요일 | 일요일 |
|---|---|---|---|---|---|---|---|
| 어디 가요? | | | | | | | |
| 왜요? | | | | | | | |

## 읽기 (Reading) 1. 토요일에 한국 문화 클럽에 가요

**케빈** 안녕, 준. 오래간만이에요.

**준** 네, 오래간만이에요. 요즘도 K-POP 댄스* 배워요?

**케빈** 네, 요즘도 친구 다섯 명하고 같이 연습해요. 준은 요즘 어떻게 지내요?

**준** 저는 매주 토요일에 한국 문화 클럽*에 가요. 아주 재미있어요. 케빈도 한국 문화 클럽*에 오세요.

**케빈** 한국 문화 클럽*에서 뭐 해요?

**준** 한국 문화를 배워요. 한국 요리하고 한국 노래도 배워요.

**케빈** 한국 문화 클럽*은 언제 해요?

**준** 한인회관에서 토요일 오전 10시에 해요. 내일 우리는 한국 영화를 봐요.

**케빈** 그래요? 그럼, 저도 같이 가요.

**준** 좋아요. 그럼, 내일 오전 9시 반에 도서관 앞에서 만나요.

*댄스: dance *클럽: club

## 읽기 (Reading) 2. 준은 아주 부지런해요.

준의 집은 서울이에요. 준의 가족은 네 명이에요. 부모님하고 누나가 한 명 있어요.
준은 오전 7시에 일어나요. 그리고 7시 30분에 아침을 먹어요.
준은 수업을 들으러 매일 학교에 가요. 준 가방에는 책 두 권하고 핸드폰하고 볼펜 세 개가 있어요.
준은 한국어 반에서 학생들을 만나요. 준은 학생들하고 같이 점심을 먹어요.
준은 토요일 오전에 한국 문화 클럽에도 가요. 한국 문화 클럽은 한인회관*에서 해요.
한국 문화 클럽에 학생들이 많이 와요. 이번 주말에 준은 한국 문화 클럽에서 한국 영화를 봐요.
그리고 일요일에 준은 커피숍에 일하러 가요. 준은 여섯 시간 일해요. 준은 아주 부지런해요.

*한인회관: Korean community centre

**연습 1** Read the narration and respond to the following questions.

1. 준은 가족이 몇 명이에요?
2. 준은 몇 시에 일어나요?
3. 준 가방에 볼펜이 몇 개 있어요?
4. 준은 일요일에 왜 커피숍에 가요?
5. 준은 몇 시간 커피숍에서 일해요?
6. 이번 주말에 준은 한국 문화 클럽에서 뭐 해요?

**연습 2** Write to describe your daily activity.

1. What time do you get up in the morning?

2. Which days do you go to school?

3. What time do you have lunch?

4. How many courses are you taking this semester? How many classes do you have today?

5. What time do you go home?

6. What time do you go to bed?

7. How many books do you have in your bag?

## 읽기 (Reading) 1. I go to the Korean cultural club on Saturday morning.

**Kevin** Hi Jun, Long time, no see.

**Jun** Yes, long time, no see. Are you still learning K-POP dancing?

**Kevin** Yes, I practice K-POP dancing with 5 friends these days. How are you doing, Jun?

**Jun** I go to the Korean cultural club every Saturday. It is fun. Please come to the club to hang out with us.

**Kevin** What do you do at the club?

**Jun** We learn Korean culture. We cook Korean food and learn Korean songs.

**Kevin** When do you go to the club?

**Jun** We go to the Korean community centre every Saturday morning at 10. We watch Korean movies tomorrow.

**Kevin** Really? Let's go there together.

**Jun** Sure, let's meet in front of the library at 9:30 am tomorrow.

## 읽기 (Reading) 2. Jun is very diligent.

Jun's hometown is Seoul. June has 4 family members. He has parents and an older sister in his family. Jun gets up at 7 am. And he eats breakfast at 7:30 am. Jun goes to school every day to attend classes. He has two books, a cellphone, and three pens in his bag. He meets students in the Korean class and has lunch together with the students. On Saturday morning, Jun also goes to the Korean culture club. They have the meeting at the Korean community centre. Many students come to the club. Jun will watch a Korean movie at the club this weekend. And on Sunday, he will go to a coffee shop to work. Jun often works for 6 hours on Sundays. He is very diligent.

## 어휘
## Vocabulary

### Nouns

| | |
|---|---|
| 강아지 | dog, puppy |
| 낮 | day |
| 노래방 | karaoke room |
| 라디오 | radio |
| 문 | door |
| 밤 | night |
| 신발 | shoes |
| 오래간만 | after a long time |
| 오전 | a.m. |
| 오후 | p.m. |
| 전화번호 | telephone number |
| 필통 | pencil case |
| 학기 [학끼] | semester |
| 핸드폰 | cellphone |

### Verbs

| | |
|---|---|
| 걷다 | to walk |
| 노래(하다) | to sing |
| 듣다 | to listen |
| 일어나다 | to get up |

### Adjectives

| | |
|---|---|
| 대단하다 | to be great, incredible |
| 멋있다 [머시따] | to be stylish |
| 부지런하다 | to be diligent |

### Counters

| | |
|---|---|
| 개 | item |
| 과목 | course |
| 권 | book |
| 년 | year |
| 달 | month (duration) |
| 달러 | dollar |
| 마리 | animal |
| 명 | people |
| 번 | number |
| 분 | minute / people (honorific) |
| 살 | age |
| 시 | hour |
| 시간 | hours |
| 원 | won |
| 월 | month (specific month) |
| 일 | day |
| 층 | floor |

### Other expressions

| | |
|---|---|
| 월요일 [워료일] | Monday |
| 화요일 | Tuesday |
| 수요일 | Wednesday |
| 목요일 [모교일] | Thursday |
| 금요일 [그묘일] | Friday |
| 토요일 | Saturday |
| 일요일 [이료일] | Sunday |
| 나중에 | later |
| 들 | plural |
| 몇 | how many |
| 언제 | when |

# Memo

# Appendices

## Answer keys

## Lesson 1

**연습 1** Let's draw the Korean national flag which is called 'Tae.gŭk.ki'.

**연습 2** Draw lines to match the names and pictures of the Korean foods.

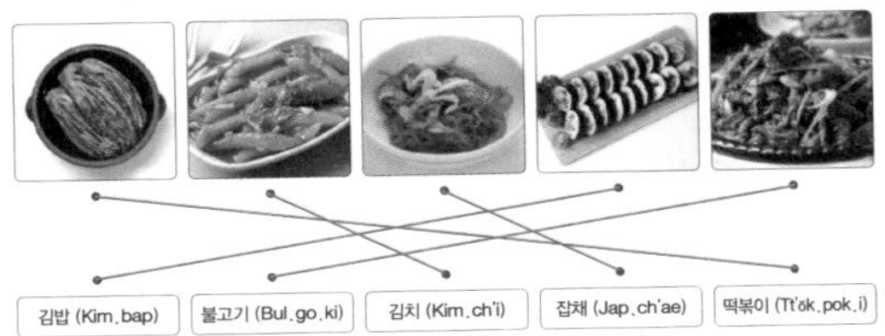


### 3. Korean syllables

**연습 7** Indicate the sound which the final of each syllable makes, as in the example.

(Example: 닫 → ㄷ)

❶ 각 ㄱ ❷ 간 ㄴ ❸ 갇 ㄷ
❹ 갈 ㄹ ❺ 감 ㅁ ❻ 갑 ㅂ
❼ 갓 ㄷ ❽ 갖 ㄷ ❾ 강 ㅇ
❿ 갗 ㄷ ⓫ 갂 ㄱ ⓬ 갈 ㄷ
⓭ 갚 ㅂ ⓮ 갛 ㄷ

**연습 16** Listen to the names of the consonants and write them in the blanks.

❶ 미음 ❷ 티읕 ❸ 시옷
❹ 디귿 ❺ 피읖 ❻ 비읍
❼ 치읓 ❽ 니은 ❾ 히읗

### 4. Pronunciation rules

**연습 1** Write the following words as they sound.

❶ 잎 [입] ❷ 곳 [곧]
❸ 맛 [맏] ❹ 빛 [빋]
❺ 꽃 [꼳] ❻ 바닥 [바닥]
❼ 기역 [기역] ❽ 서랍 [서랍]
❾ 부엌 [부억]

**연습 2** Write the following words as they sound.

❶ 연필을 [연피를] ❷ 먹었어요 [머거써요]
❸ 창문이 [창무니] ❹ 있어요 [이써요]
❺ 가을에 [가으레] ❻ 앞으로 [아프로]
❼ 들으세요 [드르세요] ❽ 집에서 [지베서]
❾ 꽃이 [꼬치] ❿ 앉으세요 [안즈세요]
⓫ 읽어요 [일거요] ⓬ 팔아서 [파라서]
⓭ 틈틈이 [틈트미] ⓮ 잠옷 [자몯]
⓯ 받았어요 [바다써요] ⓰ 할아버지 [하라버지]
⓱ 낮에 [나제] ⓲ 넓어요 [널버요]
⓳ 닦아요 [다까요]
⓴ 벤이 집에서 잠을 자고 있어요.
[베니 지베서 자믈 자고 이써요]

**연습 3** Write the following words as they sound.

❶ 같지요 [갇찌요] ❷ 깍두기 [깍뚜기]
❸ 부엌도 [부억또] ❹ 색시 [색씨]
❺ 갔다 [갇따] ❻ 밥과 [밥꽈]
❼ 낚다가 [낙따가] ❽ 몇 살 [멷쌀]
❾ 식당 [식땅] ❿ 약국 [약꾹]
⓫ 닫다 [닫따] ⓬ 학교 [학꾜]
⓭ 약국에 갔더니 약사가 있었다.
[약꾸게 갇떠니 약싸가 이썯따]

**연습 4** Write the following words as they sound.

❶ 일학년 [일항년] ❷ 이학년 [이항년]
❸ 삼학년 [삼항년 ] ❹ 사학년 [사항년]
❺ 반갑습니다 [반갑씀니다]
❻ 고맙습니다 [고맙씀니다]

**연습 5** Write the following words as they sound.

❶ 여덟 [여덜] ❷ 앉다 [안따]
❸ 많소 [만쏘] ❹ 넓다 [널따]
❺ 넓어요 [널버요] ❻ 닭 [닥]
❼ 읽다 [익따] ❽ 읽어요 [일거요]
❾ 맑다 [막따] ❿ 맑아요 [말가요]
⓫ 짧다 [짤따] ⓬ 짧아요 [짤바요]

## Lesson 2

### 발음 (Pronunciations) Review

1. Final ‘ㅂ’ is nasalized because of a neighboring nasal consonant.

반갑습니다 [반갑씀니다]
학생입니다 [학쌩임니다]

2. Final ‘ㄱ’ is nasalized into ‘ㅇ’ because of a neighboring nasal consonant.

일학년 [일항년]
이학년 [이항년]

3. When subsequent syllables do not have a consonant sound, the previous final is pronounced as the first consonant sound.

선생님은 [선생니믄]
한국어 [한구거]
사람이에요 [사라미에요]

### 문법 (Grammar) ❶

**연습 1** Write 은 or 는 after each name in the blanks.

| 줄리아는 | 준은 | 리아는 | 샤닐은 | 제니는 | 선생님은 |
|---|---|---|---|---|---|

### 문법 (Grammar) ❷

**연습 1** Complete the sentences, writing 이에요 or 예요.

| 저는 선생님 이에요 | 저는 학생 이에요 | 저는 줄리아 예요 | 저는 준 이에요 | 저는 한국 사람 이에요 |
|---|---|---|---|---|

### 읽기 (Reading) 2. 저는 서리나예요.

**연습 1** Respond to the following questions, using information from the reading above.

1. 서리나는 캐나다 사람이에요? 네, 서리나는 캐나다 사람이에요.
2. 벤은 한국어 선생님이에요? 아니요, 벤은 한국어 선생님이 아니에요. 벤은 한국어 반 학생이에요.
3. 벤도 캐나다 사람이에요? 아니요, 벤은 캐나다 사람이 아니에요. 벤은 미국 사람이에요.
4. 선생님은 친절해요? 네, 선생님은 친절해요.

## Lesson 3

### 발음 (Pronunciations) ㅎ weakening

**연습 1** Write the following according to their sound.

(Example) 전화 [저놔]

| | |
|---|---|
| 일학년 [이랑년] | 이학년 [이앙년] |
| 삼학년 [사망년] | 사학년 [사앙년] |
| 많아요 [마나요] | 사랑한다 [사랑안다] |
| 괜찮아요 [괜차나요] | 좋아요 [조아요] |
| 잘했어요 [자래써요] | 안녕하세요 [안녕아세요] |

### 문법 (Grammar) ❸

**연습 1** Complete the translation of the following sentences into Korean.

- University of Alberta has a nice library.
  → 대학교는 도서관이 좋아요.
- The school cafeteria has delicious coffee.
  → 학교 식당은 커피가 맛있어요.
- I have many friends.
  → 저는 친구가 많아요.
- The library has big desks.
  → 도서관은 책상이 커요.

### 읽기 (Reading) 2. 서리나 집은 대학교 기숙사예요.

**연습 1** The following questions are about ‘읽기 2’. Respond to the questions.

1. 서리나 집이 어디예요? 서리나 집은 기숙사예요.
2. 학교 식당이 어디 있어요? 학교 식당은 섭 빌딩 안에 있어요.
3. 학교 식당 음식이 어때요? 학교 식당 음식이 싸요. 그리고 맛있어요.
4. 서리나가 지금 뭐해요? 서리나는 지금 한국어 숙제해요.

## Lesson 4

### 발음 (Pronunciations)

맛있어요 [마시써요 / 마디써요]
맛없어요 [마덥써요]

### 문법 (Grammar) ❶

**연습 1** Complete the translation of the following sentences into Korean.

- I have a book. → 저는 책이 있어요.
- I have a banana. → 저는 바나나가 있어요.
- I have homework. → 저는 숙제가 있어요.
- Cerina has a bag. → 서리나는 가방이 있어요.
- Ben has a class. → 벤은 수업이 있어요.

**연습 3** Find the wrong part and change it to make a correct sentence.

❶ 서리나는 학생 있어요.
→ 서리나는 학생이에요.
❷ 서리나는 일학년 있어요.
→ 서리나는 일학년이에요.
❸ 서리나는 도서관이에요.
→ 서리나는 도서관에 있어요.
❹ 벤은 도서관에 이에요.
→ 벤은 도서관에 있어요.
❺ 학교 식당은 섭 빌딩에 이에요.
→ 학교 식당은 섭 빌딩에 있어요.
❻ 저는 마이클 옆에 이에요.
→ 저는 마이클 옆에 있어요.

**연습 4** Tony does not have a class today or tomorrow. He calls Ben, but he is not at home. Tony feels lonely. Read Tony's narrative and fill in the blanks with appropriate conjunctions (그리고, 그래서, or 그런데).

저는 오늘 수업이 없어요. 그래서 집에 있어요. 저는 내일도 수업이 없어요. 그래서 텔레비전을 봐요. 그런데 텔레비전이 재미없어요. 그래서 전화해요. 그런데 친구 벤이 집에 없어요. 벤은 요즘 아주 바빠요. 요즘 저는 돈도 없어요. 그래서 재미없어요. 저는 여자 친구도 없어요. 그래서 쓸쓸해요*. 냉장고에 음식도 없어요. 그래서 저는 배고파요! (*쓸쓸해요: lonely, 냉장고: refrigerator, 배고파요: hungry)

### 문법 (Grammar) ❺

**연습 1** Check all the predicates which need an object.

| 가다 | | 공부하다 | √ | 마시다 | √ | 만나다 | √ | 먹다 | √ |
|---|---|---|---|---|---|---|---|---|---|
| 보다 | √ | 아니다 | | 앉다 | | 없다 | | 예쁘다 | |
| 이다 | | 있다 | | 자다 | | 크다 | | | |

### 읽기 (Reading) 2. 한국 문화 수업

**연습 1** Read the narration and respond to the following questions.

1. 준은 뭘* 좋아해요? (*뭘: the short form of '뭐를') 준은 한국 영화를 좋아해요.
2. 누가 한국 문화 수업을 가르치세요? 권우찬 선생님이 한국 문화 수업을 가르치세요.
3. 한국 문화 수업 시간에 뭘 공부해요? 한국 문화 수업 시간에 한국 영화하고 문화를 공부해요.
4. 벤은 왜 열심히 공부해요? 벤은 한국 문화 수업을 아주 좋아해요. 그래서 열심히 공부해요.
5. 벤하고 준은 지금 어디 있어요? 벤하고 준은 지금 도서관에 있어요.

## Lesson 5

### 발음 (Pronunciations)

| | ㄱ + ㅎ/<br>ㅎ + ㄱ | ㄷ + ㅎ | ㅂ + ㅎ | ㅈ + ㅎ |
|---|---|---|---|---|
| Aspiration | ㅋ | ㅌ | ㅍ | ㅊ |
| Examples | 백화점<br>[배콰점]<br>좋고<br>[조코]<br>축하<br>[추카]<br>어떻게<br>[어떠케] | 많다<br>[만타]<br>않다<br>[안타] | 입학<br>[이팍]<br>잡히다<br>[자피다]<br>뽑히다<br>[뽀피다] | 좋지<br>[조치]<br>쌓지<br>[싸치] |

**읽기 (Reading)** 2. 서리나의 가족

**연습 1** Read the narration and respond to the following questions.

1. 서리나 가족은 어떻게 돼요? 서리나의 가족은 아버지하고 어머니하고 언니하고 남동생이 있어요.
2. 서리나 부모님은 어디 계세요? 서리나 부모님은 토론토에 계세요.
3. 서리나 어머니는 어디서 일하세요? 서리나 어머니는 도서관에서 일하세요.
4. 서리나는 오늘 뭐 해요? 서리나는 오늘 백화점에 가요.
5. 서리나는 오늘 누구 선물을 사요? 서리나는 오늘 부모님 선물을 사요.
6. 누가 대학원에서 음악을 공부해요? 서리나 언니가 대학원에서 음악을 공부해요.

## Lesson 6

**발음 (Pronunciations)** Review

1. 'ㅎ' Aspiration: 몇 학년 [며탕년]
2. Nasalization: 몇 명 [면명], 몇 마리 [면마리]
3. The pronunciation of numbers
   11 [시빌], 12 [시비], 16 [심뉵]

**읽기 (Reading)** 2. 준은 아주 부지런해요.

**연습 1** Read the narration and respond to the following questions.

1. 준은 가족이 몇 명이에요? 준은 가족이 네 명이에요.
2. 준은 몇 시에 일어나요? 준은 오전 7시에 일어나요.
3. 준 가방에 볼펜이 몇 개 있어요? 준 가방에 볼펜이 세 개 있어요.
4. 준은 일요일에 왜 커피숍에 가요? 준은 일요일에 일하러 커피숍에 가요.
5. 준은 몇 시간 커피숍에서 일해요? 준은 커피숍에서 여섯 시간 일해요.
6. 이번 주말에 준은 한국 문화 클럽에서 뭐 해요? 이번 주말에 준은 한국 문화 클럽에서 한국 영화를 봐요.

# Grammar Index

L = lesson, G = grammar

## Korean English Glossary

| Korean | English |
|---|---|
| 1(일)학년 [일항년] | first year |
| 2(이)학년 [이항년] | second year |
| 3(삼)학년 [삼항년] | third year |
| 4(사)학년 [사항년] | fourth year |
| 가게 | store |
| 가다 | to go |
| 가르치다 | to teach |
| 가방 | bag |
| 가족 | family |
| 강아지 | dog, puppy |
| 같이 [가치] | together |
| 개 | item (counter) |
| 건물 | building |
| 걷다 | to walk |
| 경제학 | economics |
| 계시다 | to be (existence) |
| 고등학생 [고등학쌩] | high school student |
| 고양이 | cat |
| 공부(하다) | to study |
| 공원 | park |
| 과 | chapter |
| 과목 | course (counter) |
| 괜찮다 [괜찬타] | to be all right |
| 교과서 | textbook |
| 교실 | classroom |
| 권 | book (counter) |
| 그거 | that |
| 그래요 | to be so |
| 그럼 | then |
| 금요일 [그묘일] | Friday |
| 기다리다 | to wait |
| 기숙사 [기숙싸] | dormitory |
| 나 (plain) | I |
| 나쁘다 | to be bad |
| 나중에 | later |
| 남동생 | younger brother |
| 남자 | man |
| 낮 | day |
| 내일 | tomorrow |
| 네 | Yes |
| 넓다 [널따] | to be spacious |
| 년 | year (counter) |
| 노래방 | karaoke room |
| 노래(하다) | to sing |
| 누구 | who |
| 누굴 (누구를) | who |
| 누나 | the older sister of a male |
| 다시 | again |
| 달 | month (counter – duration) |
| 달러 | dollar (counter) |
| 대단하다 | to be great, incredible |
| 대학교 [대학꾜] | college, university |
| 대학원생 [대하권생] | graduate student |
| 대학생 [대학쌩] | university student |
| 도서관 | library |
| 돈 | money |
| 동생 | younger sibling |
| 동아시아학 | East Asian studies |
| 되다 | to become |
| 뒤 | the back |
| 듣다 | to listen |
| 들 | plural |
| 들어오다 | to come in |
| 똑똑 | knock, knock! |
| 라디오 | radio |
| 마리 | animal (counter) |
| 마시다 | to drink |
| 만 | only |
| 만나다 | to meet |
| 많다 [만타] | to be many |
| 많이 | a lot |
| 말다 (마세요) | to stop |
| 맛없다 [마덥따] | to be not tasty |
| 맛있다 | to be delicious |
| 매일 | every day |
| 먹다 | to eat |
| 멋있다 [머시따] | to be stylish |
| 명 | people (counter) |
| 몇 | how many |
| 모자 | hat |
| 목요일 [모교일] | Thursday |
| 무엇/뭐 | what |

| | |
|---|---|
| 문 | door |
| 문화 | culture |
| 물 | water |
| 뭘 (뭐를) | what |
| 미국 | America |
| 밑 | the bottom |
| 바쁘다 | to be busy |
| 반 | class |
| 반갑다 (반가워요) | to be glad |
| 밤 | night |
| 밥 | meal |
| 방 | room |
| 배우다 | to learn |
| 백화점 [배콰점] | department store |
| 번 | number (counter) |
| 보다 | to see, look, watch |
| 보통 | usually |
| 볼펜 | ball-point pen |
| 부모님 | parents |
| 부지런하다 | to be diligent |
| 분 | minute (counter) /people (counter – honorific) |
| 비싸다 | to be expensive |
| 빌딩 | building |
| 빵 | bread |
| 사과 | apple |
| 사다 | to buy |
| 사람 | person |
| 사이 | relationship |
| 사전 | dictionary |
| 살 | age (counter) |
| 생일 | birthday |
| 서점 | bookstore |
| 선물 | present, gift |
| 선생님 | teacher |
| 쇼핑(하다) | to shop |
| 수업 | class |
| 수영(하다) | to swim |
| 수요일 | Wednesday |
| 숙제(하다) [숙쩨하다] | to do homework |
| 시 | hour (counter) |
| 시간 | (1) time (2) hours (counter) |
| 시계 | watch, clock |
| 시험 | test, exam |
| 식당 [식땅] | restaurant |
| 신발 | shoes |
| 싸다 | to be cheap |
| 아니다 (아니에요) | not to be |
| 아니요 | No |
| 아버지 | father |
| 아주 | very |
| 아침 | breakfast, morning |
| 안 | the inside |
| 안녕하다 (안녕하세요) | hello |
| 앉다 | to sit |
| 알다 | to know |
| 어떻게 [어떠케] | how |
| 언니 | the older sister of a female |
| 언제 | when |
| 없다 | (1) to not be (existence) (2) to not have |
| 여동생 | younger sister |
| 여자 | woman |
| 연구실 | professor's office |
| 연습하다 [연스파다] | to practice |
| 연필 | pencil |
| 열심히 [열씨미] | hard/deligently |
| 영국 | England |
| 영화 | movie |
| 영화관 | movie theatre |
| 오늘 | today |
| 오다 | to come |
| 오래간만 | after a long time |
| 오빠 | the older brother of a female |
| 오전 | a.m. |
| 오후 | p.m. |
| 옷 | clothes |
| 왜 | why |
| 요리(하다) | to cook |
| 요즘 | these days |
| 우리 | we |
| 우산 | umbrella |
| 우체국 | post office |
| 운동(하다) | to exercise |
| 원 | won (Korean currency) |
| 월 | month (counter – specific month) |

| | |
|---|---|
| 월요일 [워료일] | Monday |
| 위 | the upper |
| 음식 | food |
| 음악 [으막] | music |
| 의자 | chair |
| 이거 | this |
| 이다 (이에요/예요) | to be |
| 이름 | name |
| 이번 | this time |
| 이야기(하다) | to talk |
| 인사(하다) | to greet |
| 일 | day (counter) |
| 일본 | Japan |
| 일어나다 | to get up |
| 일요일 [이료일] | Sunday |
| 일(하다) | to work |
| 읽다 [익따] | to read |
| 있다 | (1) to be (existence)<br>(2) to have |
| 자다 | to sleep |
| 작다 | to be small (size) |
| 잘 | well |
| 재미없다 | to be uninteresting |
| 재미있다 | to be interesting |
| 저 (humble) | I |
| 저거 | that |
| 저녁 | supper, evening |
| 전공 | major |
| 전화번호 | telephone number |
| 전화(하다) | to call |
| 점심 | lunch |
| 조금 | a little |
| 좀 | a little |
| 좋다 [조타] | to be good |
| 좋아하다 | to like |
| 주다 | to give |
| 주말 | weekend |
| 주스 | juice |
| 중국 | China |
| 지갑 | wallet |
| 지금 | now |
| 지내다 | to get along |
| 지우개 | eraser |
| 질문 | question |
| 집 | house, home |
| 차 | tea |
| 책 | book |
| 책상 [책쌍] | desk |
| 체육관 [체육꽌] | gym |
| 층 | floor (counter) |
| 치다 | to play (tennis) |
| 친구 | friend |
| 친절하다 | to be kind |
| 친척 | relative |
| 칠판 | blackboard |
| 캐나다 | Canada |
| 커피 | coffee |
| 커피숍 | coffee shop |
| 컴퓨터 | computer |
| 크다 | to be big |
| 테니스 | tennis |
| 토요일 | Saturday |
| 텔레비전 | television |
| 필통 | pencil case |
| 하다 | to do |
| 학교 [학꾜] | school |
| 학기 [학끼] | semester |
| 학생 [학쌩] | student |
| 한국 | Korea |
| 한국어 [한구거] | Korean language |
| 한 번 | one time (frequency) |
| 할아버지 [하라버지] | grandfather |
| 할머니 | grandmother |
| 핸드폰 | cellphone |
| 형 | the older brother of a male |
| 형제 | siblings |
| 화요일 | Tuesday |

# English Korean Glossary

| English | Korean |
|---|---|
| after a long time | 오래간만 |
| a.m. | 오전 |
| America | 미국 |
| again | 다시 |
| age (counter) | 살 |
| and | 그리고 |
| animal (counter) | 마리 |
| apple | 사과 |
| a lot | 많이 |
| at | 에 |
| back | 뒤 |
| bad | 나쁘다 |
| bag | 가방 |
| ball-point pen | 볼펜 |
| be (existence) | 있다 |
| be (existence) | 계시다 (honorific) |
| be (identification) | 이다 |
| be all right, okay | 괜찮다 |
| be so | 그래요 |
| become | 되다 |
| big | 크다 |
| birthday | 생일 |
| blackboard | 칠판 |
| book | 책 |
| book (counter) | 권 |
| bookstore | 서점 |
| bottom | 밑 |
| bread | 빵 |
| breakfast | 아침 |
| building | 빌딩/건물 |
| busy | 바쁘다 |
| but | 그런데 |
| buy | 사다 |
| call | 전화(하다) |
| Canada | 캐나다 |
| cat | 고양이 |
| cellphone | 핸드폰 |
| chair | 의자 |
| chapter (counter) | 과 |
| cheap | 싸다 |
| China | 중국 |
| class | 반 |
| classroom | 교실 |
| clock | 시계 |
| clothes | 옷 |
| coffee | 커피 |
| coffee shop | 커피숍 |
| come | 오다 |
| come in | 들어오다 |
| computer | 컴퓨터 |
| cook | 요리(하다) |
| course (counter) | 과목 |
| culture | 문화 |
| day | 낮 |
| day (counter) | 일 |
| delicious | 맛있다 |
| department store | 백화점 |
| desk | 책상 |
| dictionary | 사전 |
| diligent | 부지런하다 |
| diligently | 열심히 |
| dog | 강아지, 개 |
| dollar (counter) | 달러 |
| door | 문 |
| dormitory | 기숙사 |
| drink | 마시다 |
| East Asian studies | 동아시아학 |
| eat | 먹다 |
| economics | 경제학 |
| England | 영국 |
| English | 영어 |
| eraser | 지우개 |
| evening | 저녁 |
| every day | 매일 |
| exam | 시험 |
| exercise | 운동(하다) |
| expensive | 비싸다 |
| family | 가족 |
| father | 아버지 |
| floor (counter) | 층 |
| first year | 1(일)학년 |
| Friday | 금요일 |

| | |
|---|---|
| friend | 친구 |
| front | 앞 |
| food | 음식 |
| fourth year | 4(사)학년 |
| get along | 지내다 |
| get up | 일어나다 |
| gift | 선물 |
| give | 주다 |
| glad | 반갑다 |
| go | 가다 |
| good | 좋다 |
| graduate student | 대학원생 |
| grandfather | 할아버지 |
| grandmother | 할머니 |
| great | 대단하다 |
| greet | 인사(하다) |
| gym | 체육관 |
| have (possession) | 있다 |
| hat | 모자 |
| hello | 안녕하다 |
| high school student | 고등학생 |
| home | 집 |
| homework | 숙제(하다) |
| hour (counter) | 시 |
| hours (counter) | 시간 |
| house | 집 |
| how | 어떻다/어떻게 |
| how many | 몇 |
| I | 나(plain)/저(humble) |
| inside | 안 |
| interesting | 재미있다 |
| item (counter) | 개 |
| Japan | 일본 |
| juice | 주스 |
| karaoke room | 노래방 |
| kind | 친절하다 |
| knock (sound) | 똑똑 |
| know | 알다 |
| Korea | 한국 |
| Korean language | 한국어 |
| later | 나중에 |
| learn | 배우다 |
| lesson | 과 |
| library | 도서관 |

| | |
|---|---|
| like | 좋아하다 |
| listen | 듣다 |
| little | 좀/ 조금 |
| look | 보다 |
| lunch | 점심 |
| major | 전공 |
| man | 남자 |
| many | 많다 |
| meal | 밥 |
| meet | 만나다 |
| minute (counter) | 분 |
| Monday | 월요일 |
| money | 돈 |
| month (counter) | 달, 월 |
| morning | 아침 |
| mother | 어머니 |
| movie | 영화 |
| movie theatre | 영화관 |
| music | 음악 |
| name | 이름 |
| night | 밤 |
| no | 아니요 |
| not be (existence) | 없다 |
| not be (neg. equation) | 아니다 |
| not have (possession) | 없다 |
| not tasty | 맛없다 |
| now | 지금 |
| number (counter) | 번호 |
| office (professor's) | 연구실 |
| older brother of a female | 오빠 |
| older brother of a male | 형 |
| older sister of a male | 누나 |
| older sister of a female | 언니 |
| one time (frequency) | 한 번 |
| only | 만 |
| outside | 밖 |
| parents | 부모님 |
| park | 공원 |
| pencil | 연필 |
| pencil case | 필통 |
| people (counter) | 명 |
| people (hon. counter) | 분 |
| person | 사람 |
| play (tennis) | (테니스를) 치다 |

| | |
|---|---|
| plural | 들 |
| p.m. | 오후 |
| practice | 연습(하다) |
| post office | 우체국 |
| present | 선물 |
| question | 질문 |
| radio | 라디오 |
| read | 읽다 |
| relationship | 사이 |
| relative | 친척 |
| restaurant | 식당 |
| room | 방 |
| Saturday | 토요일 |
| school | 학교 |
| second year | 2(이)학년 |
| see | 보다 |
| semester | 학기 |
| shoes | 신발 |
| shop | 쇼핑(하다) |
| siblings | 형제 |
| side | 옆 |
| sing | 노래(하다) |
| sit | 앉다 |
| small (size) | 작다 |
| so | 그래서 |
| spacious | 넓다 |
| stop | 말다/마세요(honorific) |
| store | 가게 |
| student | 학생 |
| study | 공부하다 |
| stylish | 멋있다 |
| Sunday | 일요일 |
| supper | 저녁 |
| swim | 수영하다 |
| tea | 차 |
| teach | 가르치다 |
| teacher | 선생님 |
| telephone number | 전화번호 |
| television | 텔레비전 |
| tennis | 테니스 |
| test | 시험 |
| textbook | 교과서 |
| that one | 그거/저거 |
| then | 그럼 |
| these days | 요즘 |
| third year | 3(삼)학년 |
| this one | 이거 |
| this time | 이번 |
| time | 시간 |
| Thursday | 목요일 |
| today | 오늘 |
| together | 같이 |
| tomorrow | 내일 |
| Tuesday | 화요일 |
| umbrella | 우산 |
| uninteresting | 재미없다 |
| university | 대학교 |
| university student | 대학생 |
| upper | 위 |
| usually | 보통 |
| very | 아주 |
| wait | 기다리다 |
| wallet | 지갑 |
| walk | 걷다 |
| watch | 시계 |
| water | 물 |
| we | 우리/저희(humble) |
| Wednesday | 수요일 |
| weekend | 주말 |
| well | 잘 |
| what | 무엇/뭐/뭘 |
| when | 언제 |
| where | 어디 |
| who | 누구/누구를/누굴 |
| why | 왜 |
| woman | 여자 |
| won (counter) | 원 |
| work | 일(하다) |
| year (counter) | 년 |
| yes | 네 |
| younger brother | 남동생 |
| younger sibling | 동생 |
| younger sister | 여동생 |

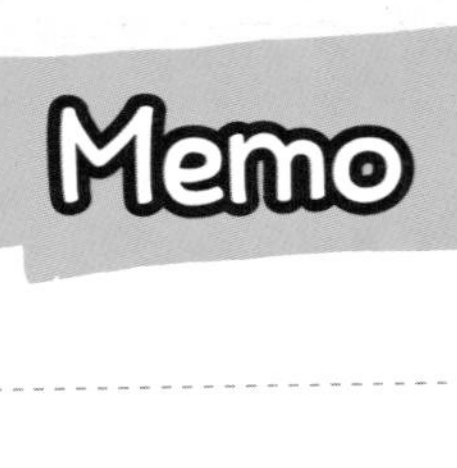
Memo

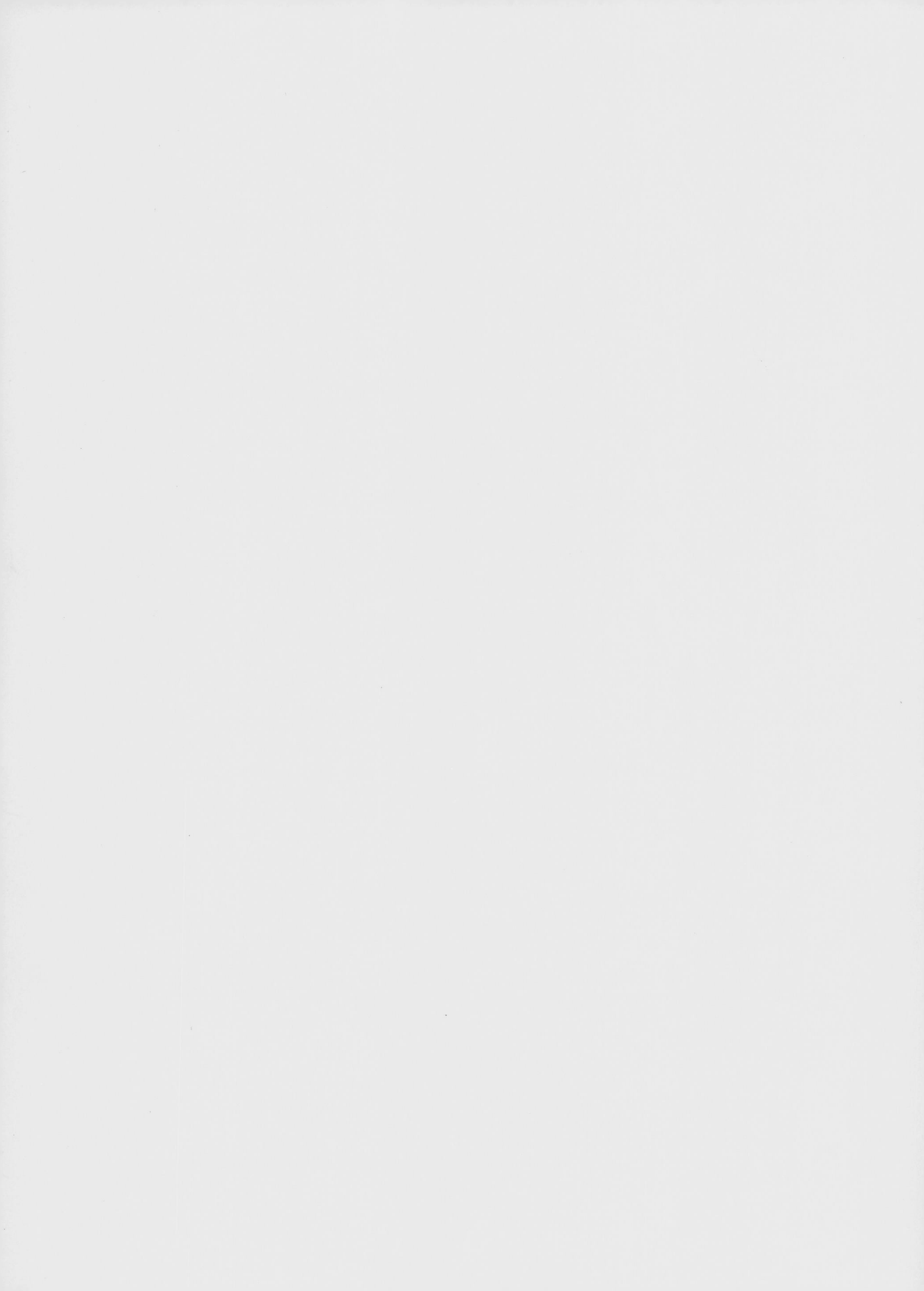